AEROFILMS GUIDE

FOOTBALL GROUNDS

NINTH REVISED EDITION

C000258527

AEROFILMS GUIDE
FOOTBALL GROUNDS
NINTH REVISED EDITION

DIAL
HOUSE

CONTENTS

Front cover: With the ongoing saga of the redevelopment of Wembley Stadium showing no sign of being concluded, England's national team has been forced to play home matches in a number of provincial stadia. For Cup and Play-Off finals, the Millennium Stadium in Cardiff, illustrated here, has been selected as the venue. Whilst there have been concerns about the state of the pitch, it remains true that this successor to Cardiff Arms Park is an impressive structure.

Back cover: With its capacity now exceeding 50,000 Newcastle United's St James' Park is without doubt one of the most impressive of Premiership grounds. Dominating the landscape, the ground is almost impossible to miss when travelling to the city from the south.

Preceding pages: Manchester United and Rushden & Diamonds are two of the most ambitious football teams in the country; the varying scales of the grounds possessed by a team bent on dominating Europe and one entering the Nationwide League for the first time are all too apparent in this pair of photographs. Old Trafford has a capacity of 67,000 whilst Nene Park has barely a tenth of that figure.

First published in 1993; Reprinted 1993 (twice); Second edition 1994; Third edition 1995; Fourth edition 1996; Fifth edition 1997; Sixth edition 1998; Seventh edition 1999; Eighth edition 2000; Ninth edition 2001.

ISBN 0 7110 2838 9

All rights reserved. No part of this book may be reproduced or transmitted in any form or by any means, electronic or mechanical, including photocopying, recording or by any information storage and retrieval system, without permission from the Publisher in writing.

Published by Dial Hose
an imprint of Ian Allan Publishing Ltd, Terminal House, Shepperton, Surrey TW17 8AS; and printed by Ian Allan Printing Ltd, Riverdene Business Park, Hersham, Surrey KT12 4RG.

Code: 01/08E

Text © Ian Allan Publishing Ltd 1993-2001
Diagrams © Ian Allan Publishing Ltd 2000-1
Aerial Photography © Aerofilms

Aerofilms Limited have been specialists in aerial photography since 1919. Their library of aerial photographs, both new and old, is in excess of 1.5 million images. Aerofilms undertake to commission oblique and vertical survey aerial photography, which is processed and printed in their specialised photographic laboratory. Digital photomaps are prepared using precision scanners.

Free photostatic proofs are available on request for any site held within the collection and price lists will be forwarded detailing the size of photographic enlargement available without any obligation to purchase.

Introduction

Welcome to the ninth edition of *Aerofilms Guide: Football Grounds* — the first edition to be published in the new millennium. Perhaps appropriately, the first new ground to be featured in this year's edition is the Millennium Stadium in Cardiff, a ground which will be much used over the next few years as Wembley is — probably — redeveloped. The saga of the rebuilding of England's national stadium is not an edifying one and one that reflects poorly on all involved in the process. Given the huge amount of money in contemporary football it does seem extraordinary that the project can have got itself into the apparent mess that it is. The costs may be prohibitive, but when Premiership teams like Arsenal can contemplate spending £250 million on a new league ground — just under half of the anticipated budget for the new Wembley — it does seem peculiar that those behind the project cannot get their collective act together.

Apart from the Millennium Stadium, two other completely new grounds are featured this year: Southampton's new home and Rushden & Diamonds. For many years The Dell represented the smallest ground in the Premiership, a fact which undoubtedly undermined Southampton's attempts to retain top-flight status. With the new ground now ready, doubling the potential gate, the Saints will no longer be at such a disadvantage. However, cynics will note that many teams that move into new stadia suddenly discover life in a lower division. A third new ground, Oxford United's Kassam Stadium, seems to have been in development so long that it is almost a familiar friend.

For Rushden & Diamonds, Nationwide League football has been long on the agenda for one of the most ambitious teams in the non-league divisions. For several years the team has been close to achieving league status; in 2000/01 this was finally achieved and the club's well appointed stadium will put many in the Third Division (and higher) to shame.

Elsewhere, major work continues at a number of grounds and wherever possible this work has been recorded. Contemporary construction methods, however, often mean that work which was started after our press dates can appear ready for use by the start of the new season. Major developments this year to note include new or expanded stands at, for example, Bradford City, Charlton Athletic and Ipswich Town and the process of relocation and expansion sees no end, with new grounds again proposed for Leicester City and many others.

As always, we end this introduction with a hope that you will have an enjoyable season and that your team will have the success that every fan hopes for.

Disabled Facilities

We endeavour to list the facilities for disabled spectators at each ground. Readers will appreciate that these facilities can vary in number and quality and that, for most clubs, pre-booking is essential. Some clubs also have dedicated parking for disabled spectators; this again should be pre-booked if available.

MILLENNIUM STADIUM

Westgate Street, Cardiff CF10 1JA

Tel No: 029 2023 2661
Fax: 029 2023 2678
Stadium Tours: 02920 822228
Web Site: www.millenniumstadium-plc.co.uk
Brief History: The stadium, built upon the site of the much-loved and historic Cardiff Arms Park, was opened in 2000 and cost in excess of £100 million (a tiny sum in comparison with the current forecast spend — if it happens — of over £600 million on the redevelopment of Wembley). As the national stadium for Wales, the ground will be primarily used in sporting terms by Rugby Union, but will be used by the FA to host major fixtures (such as FA Cup and Worthington Cup finals) until, in theory, 2004 when the new Wembley was scheduled for completion.

(Total) Current Capacity: 72,500
Nearest Railway Station: Cardiff Central
Parking (Car): Street parking only.
Parking (Coach/Bus): As directed by the police
Police Force and Tel No: South Wales (029 2022 2111)
Disabled Visitors' Facilities:
  Wheelchairs: c250 designated seats. The whole stadium has been designed for ease of disabled access with lifts, etc.
  Blind: Commentary available.
Anticipated Development(s): None planned

KEY

↑ North direction (approx)

❶ Cardiff Central station
❷ Bus station
❸ River Taff
❹ Castle Street
❺ Westgate Street
❻ Wood Street
❼ Tudor Street
❽ High Street
❾ St Mary Street
❿ To Cardiff Queen Street station

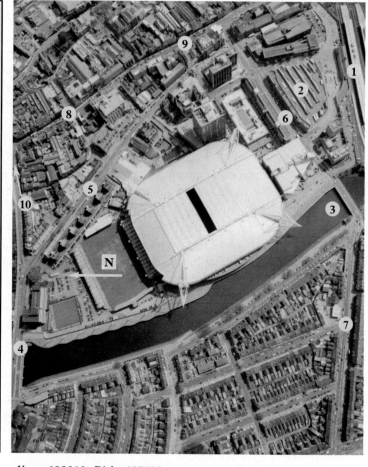

Above: 688019; *Right:* 687998

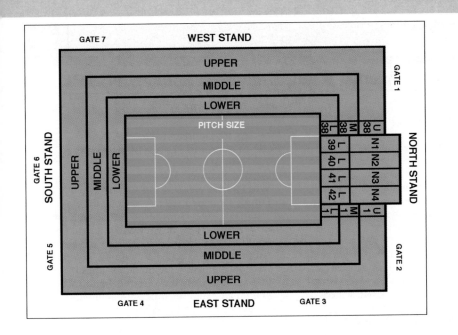

WEST STAND

GATE 7

GATE 1

UPPER		
MIDDLE		
LOWER		

PITCH SIZE

GATE 6 · SOUTH STAND

UPPER	MIDDLE	LOWER

U 38	M 38	L 38
	L 39	N1
	L 40	N2
	L 41	N3
	L 42	N4
U 1	M 1	L 1

NORTH STAND

GATE 2

LOWER

MIDDLE

UPPER

GATE 5

GATE 4   **EAST STAND**   GATE 3

ARSENAL

Arsenal Stadium, Avenell Road, Highbury, London, N5 1BU

Tel No: 020 7704 4000
Advance Tickets Tel No: 020 7704 4040
Fax: 020 7704 4001
Web Site: www.arsenal.co.uk
League: F.A. Premier
Brief History: Founded 1886 as Royal Arsenal, changed to Woolwich Arsenal in 1891, and Arsenal in 1914. Former grounds: Plumstead Common, Sportsman Ground, Manor Ground (twice), moved to Arsenal Stadium (Highbury) in 1913. Record attendance 73,295
(Total) Current Capacity: 38,900 (all seated)
Visiting Supporters' Allocation: 2,900 (all seated Clock End and Lower Tier West Stand)
Club Colours: Red shirts with white sleeves, white shorts
Nearest Railway Station: Drayton Park or Finsbury Park (main line). Arsenal (tube)
Parking (Car): Street Parking
Parking (Coach/Bus): Drayton Park
Police Force and Tel No: Metropolitan (020 7263 9090)
Disabled Visitors' Facilities:
  Wheelchairs: Lower tier East Stand
  Blind: Commentary available
Anticipated Development(s): The club has now confirmed its intention to construct a new 60,000-seat stadium on a 25-acre site at Ashpurton Grove. It is hoped that work will start on the new £250 million stadium, subject to planning permission from Islington Council, in about 12 months time with completion for the start of the 2004/05 season.

KEY

C Club Offices
S Club Shop
E Entrance(s) for visiting supporters

↑ North direction (approx)

❶ Avenell Road
❷ Highbury Hill
❸ Gillespie Road
❹ To Drayton Park BR Station (1/4 mile)
❺ Arsenal Tube Station
❻ Clock End
❼ St Thomas's Road (to Finsbury Park station)
❽ North Bank
❾ West Stand
❿ East Stand

Above: 688318; *Right:* 688311

Another season in which the Gunners finished as runners up to Manchester United — but still at a considerable distance behind the champions — proved that Arsene Wenger's team remains the best of the also-rans. Failure to match United in the Premiership was, however, mitigated by a further FA Cup final appearance against Liverpool — having defeated Tottenham in the semi-finals — and by reasonable progress in the Champions League, where the team was defeated in the quarter-finals on the away goals rule by Spanish team Valencia. At times, Arsenal produced some stunning football — as you'd expect from a team including players like Henry and Kanu — but all too often the side failed to produce the goods against lower teams. If Arsenal are to sustain a meaningful challenge in 2001/02, then they'll need to be much more ruthless than in previous years.

ASTON VILLA

Villa Park, Trinity Road, Birmingham, B6 6HE

Tel No: 0121 327 2299
Advance Tickets Tel No: 0121 327 5353
Fax: 0121 322 2107
Web Site: www.avfc.co.uk
E-Mail: postmaster@astonvilla-fc.co.uk
League: F.A. Premier
Brief History: Founded in 1874. Founder Members Football League (1888). Former Grounds: Aston Park and Lower Aston Grounds and Perry Bar, moved to Villa Park (a development of the Lower Aston Grounds) in 1897. Record attendance 76,588
(Total) Current Capacity: 43,000 (all seated) (Prior to redevelopment)
Visiting Supporters' Allocation: Approx 2,983 in North Stand

Club Colours: Claret with blue stripe shirts, claret shorts
Nearest Railway Station: Witton
Parking (Car): Asda car park, Aston Hall Road
Parking (Coach/Bus): Asda car park, Aston Hall Road (special coach park for visiting supporters situated in Witton Lane)
Police Force and Tel No: West Midlands (0121 322 6010)
Disabled Visitors' Facilities:
   Wheelchairs: Trinity Road Stand section
   Blind: Commentary by arrangement
Anticipated Development(s): With the completion of the new Trinity Road Stand, the redevelopment of Villa Park is now complete.

KEY

C Club Offices
S Club Shop
E Entrance(s) for visiting supporters
R Refreshment bars for visiting supporters
T Toilets for visiting supporters

↑ North direction (approx)

❶ B4137 Witton Lane
❷ B4140 Witton Road
❸ Trinity Road
❹ A4040 Aston Lane to A34 Walsall Road
❺ To Aston Expressway & M6
❻ Holte End
❼ Visitors' Car Park
❽ To Witton railway station (100yd)
❾ North Stand
❿ Trinity Road Stand

Above: 688331; *Right:* 688329

With the new Trinity Road Stand being completed during the year, allowing Villa Park to stage an international friendly after the demise of Wembley, the ground is certainly now an impressive one. Unfortunately, however, the team on the field never really prospered on the field; an early season foray into the Intertoto Cup proved a pointless exercise as Villa failed to progress into the UEFA Cup, whilst domestically a squad — including the mercurial David Ginola — that promised much failed to deliver more than a mid-table position in the Premiership. A perceived lack of ambition led to increasing player dissatisfaction, with a number of prominent players (such as Gareth Southgate) wishing to depart and increasing tension between the management and certain others. The new season could well see John Gregory's position under threat unless the team starts quickly to challenge for honours.

BARNSLEY

Oakwell Ground, Grove Street, Barnsley, S71 1ET

Tel No: 01226 211211
Advance Tickets Tel No: 01226 211211
Fax: 01226 211444
Web Site: www.barnsleyfc.co.uk
E-mail: thereds@barnsleyfc.co.uk
League: 1st Division
Brief History: Founded in 1887 as Barnsley St Peter's, changed name to Barnsley in 1897. Former Ground: Doncaster Road, Worsboro Bridge until 1888. Record attendance 40,255
(Total) Current Capacity: 23,009 (all seated)
Visiting Supporters' Allocation: 6,000 maximum (all seated; North Stand)
Club Colours: Red shirts, white shorts
Nearest Railway Station: Barnsley Exchange
Parking (Car): Queen's Ground car park

Parking (Coach/Bus): Queen's Ground car park
Police Force and Tel No: South Yorkshire (01266 206161)
Disabled Visitors' Facilities:
  Wheelchairs: Purpose Built Disabled Stand
  Blind: Commentary available
Future Development(s): With the completion of the new North Stand with its 6,000 capacity, the next phase for the redevelopment of Oakwell will feature the old West Stand with its remaining open seating. There is, however, no timescale for this work.

KEY

C Club Offices
S Club Shop
E Entrance(s) for visiting supporters

↑ North direction (approx)

❶ A628 Pontefract Road
❷ To Barnsley Exchange BR station and M1 Junction 37 (two miles)
❸ Queen's Ground Car Park
❹ North Stand
❺ Grove Street
❻ To Town Centre

Above: 685529; Right: 685527

There were high hopes at Oakwell at the start of the season, given the team's success in reaching the Play-Offs at the end of 1999/2000 and, under Dave Bassett, the team had a manager with a good track record in bringing success. In the event, however, 2000/01 will be one season in recent years that fans will want to forget. Poor results during the first few months of the season led to Bassett's dismissal during December and under new manager Nigel Spackman the team's performances improved, with the final mid-table position being considerably better than it seemed the club would achieve before Bassett's departure. However, with the Premiership 'parachute' now expired and with a number of highly ambitious teams in the First Division, it will be a hard struggle for Barnsley to threaten even a Play-Off position in 2001/02.

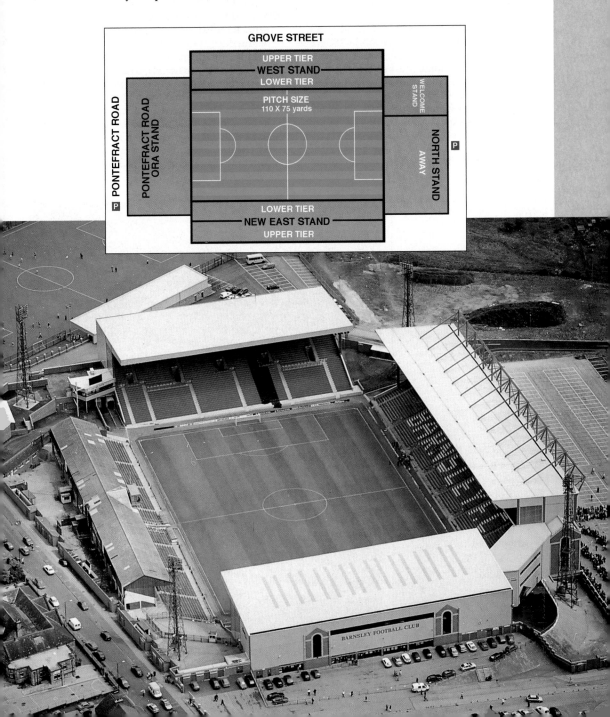

BIRMINGHAM CITY

St Andrew's, St Andrew's Street, Birmingham, B9 4NH

Tel No: 0121 772 0101
Advance Tickets Tel No: 0121 772 0101
Fax: 0121 766 7866
Web Site: www.bcfc.com
League: 1st Division
Brief History: Founded 1875, as Small Heath Alliance. Changed to Small Heath in 1888, Birmingham in 1905, Birmingham City in 1945. Former Grounds: Arthur Street, Ladypool Road, Muntz Street, moved to St Andrew's in 1906. Record attendance 68,844
(Total) Current Capacity: 30,016 (all seated)
Visiting Supporters' Allocation: 1-4,500 in new Railway End (Lower Tier)
Club Colours: Blue shirts, white shorts
Nearest Railway Station: Birmingham New Street

Parking (Car): Street parking
Parking (Coach/Bus): Coventry Road
Police Force and Tel No: West Midlands (0121 772 1169)
Disabled Visitors' Facilities:
  Wheelchairs: 90 places; advanced notice required
  Blind: Commentary available
Future Development(s): With the completion of the rebuilding of the Railway End, attention has turned to the old Main Stand. There are proposals for the construction of a 7,500-seat stand, which would also incorporate a hotel and conference centre. There is no definite time scale for this project, which would conclude the rebuilding of St Andrews.

KEY

C Club Offices
S Club Shop
E Entrance(s) for visiting supporters

↑ North direction (approx)

❶ Car Park
❷ B4128 Cattell Road
❸ Tilton Road
❹ Garrison Lane
❺ To A4540 & A38 (M)
❻ To City Centre and New Street BR Station (1½ miles)
❼ Railway End
❽ Tilton Road End
❾ Main Stand
❿ Kop Stand
⓫ Emmeline Street
⓬ Kingston Road
⓭ St Andrew's Street

14   *Above: 679483; Right:* 679479

CATTELL ROAD

KOP STAND

DISABLED FANS

PITCH SIZE
115 X 75 yards

TILTON ROAD

TILTON ROAD END

RAILWAY END
AWAY

DISABLED FANS

OLYMPIC GALLERY

EMMELINE STREET

DISABLED FANS

MAIN STAND

ST ANDREW'S STREET

Again, another season of frustration for Trevor Francis and Birmingham City. Challenging for automatic promotion for almost the duration and achieving, yet again, a Play-Off spot, the team was to be defeated under controversial circumstances in the Play-Offs by the surprise package of the First Division in 2000/01, Preston North End. With the scores level after extra time at Deepdale, the Play-Off semi-final was determined by penalties. As one end of Deepdale was under reconstruction, the penalties were taken into the end occupied by home fans, much to Francis's obvious anger. However, the result stood and City was consigned to another season of First Division football. So far the board at St Andrew's has been supportive of Francis but one suspects that, sooner or later, patience will be exhausted and new blood brought in. Will 2001/02 be Francis's last hurrah at the Blues?

BLACKBURN ROVERS

Ewood Park, Blackburn, Lancashire, BB2 4JF

Tel No: 01254 698888
Advance Tickets Tel No: 01254 671666
Fax: 01254 671042
Web Site: www.rovers.co.uk
E-Mail: enquiries@rovers.co.uk
League: FA Premier
Brief History: Founded 1875. Former Grounds: Oozebooth, Pleasington Cricket Ground, Alexandra Meadows. Moved to Ewood Park in 1890. Founder members of Football League (1888). Record attendance 61,783
(Total) Current Capacity: 31,367 (all seated)
Visiting Supporters' Allocation: 3,914 at the Darwen End

Club Colours: Blue and white halved shirts, white shorts
Nearest Railway Station: Blackburn
Parking (Car): Street parking
Parking (Coach/Bus): As directed by Police
Police Force and Tel No: Lancashire (01254 51212)
Disabled Visitors' Facilities:
  Wheelchairs: All sides of the ground
  Blind: Commentary available
Anticipated Development(s): There is talk that the Walkersteel Stand may be rebuilt, but this is very tentative at this stage.

KEY

C Club Offices
S Club Shop
E Entrance(s) for visiting supporters
R Refreshment bars for visiting supporters
T Toilets for visiting supporters

↑ North direction (approx)

❶ A666 Bolton Road
❷ Kidder Street
❸ Nuttall Street
❹ Town Centre & Blackburn Central BR station (1½ miles)
❺ To Darwen and Bolton
❻ Car parking area for 500 cars
❼ Car Parks
❽ Top O'Croft Road

The last season was one both of sadness and of joy for the Rovers' faithful: sadness at the start of the season with the death of long-term benefactor Jack Walker turning to joy at the end with automatic promotion back to the Premiership after two years in the First Division. Despite the undoubted skills of the squad, however, it looked for several months as if Graeme Souness's team would fail to make an impact on what was potentially a strong First Division. It was only after October that the points started to flow and automatic promotion was guaranteed with a win over Preston North End on 2 May. Blackburn are probably a stronger team than the three that have been relegated; none the less, it is becoming evident that the gap between First Division and Premiership is growing, particularly in financial terms, and fans will be hoping that Rovers emulate recent successes Sunderland, Ipswich and Charlton, rather than Manchester City, Watford and Bradford City.

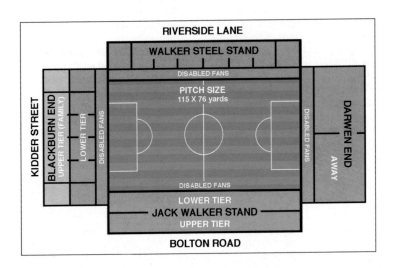

BLACKPOOL

Bloomfield Road, Blackpool, Lancashire, FY1 6JJ

Tel No: 01253 405331
Advance Tickets Tel No: 01253 404331
Fax: 01253 405011
E-Mail: info@blackpoolfc.co.uk
Web Site: www.blackpoolfc.co.uk
League: 2nd Division
Brief History: Founded 1887, merged with
'South Shore' (1899). Former grounds: Raikes
Hall (twice) and Athletic Grounds, Stanley
Park, South Shore played at Cow Cap Lane,
moved to Bloomfield Road in 1899. Record
attendance 38,098
(Total) Current Capacity: 6,100 (1,521 seated)
Visiting Supporters' Allocation: 1,040
Club Colours: Tangerine shirts, white shorts
Nearest Railway Station: Blackpool South
Parking (Car): At Ground and street parking
(also behind West Stand – from M55)

Parking (Coach/Bus): Mecca car park (behind
North End (also behind West Stand –
from M55)
Police Force and Tel No: Lancashire (01253
293933)
Disabled Visitors' Facilities:
Wheelchairs: By players entrance
Blind: Commentary available (limited
numbers)
Anticipated Development(s): Although work
on the demolition of the Kop End and old
Main Stand was completed before the start of
the 2000/01 season, work on their
replacements was delayed until towards the
end of the season. Work on the £10.7 million
project will be completed by November 2001.

KEY	
C	Club Offices
S	Club Shop
E	Entrance(s) for visiting supporters
R	Refreshment bars for visiting supporters
T	Toilets for visiting supporters

↑ North direction (approx)

❶ Car Park
❷ To Blackpool South BR Station (1½ miles) and M55 Junction 4
❸ Bloomfield Drive
❹ Central Drive
❺ Henry Street
❻ East Paddock
❼ South Stand

Above: 688056a; Right: 688051

Following relegation at the end of 1999/2000, the Seasiders started the new campaign in the Third Division with a half-demolished ground and a team under the management of Steve Macmahon. Although the club's league form resulted in the team reaching the Play-Offs, the season was not without its downside — losing to Conference team Yeovil in the FA Cup was an undoubted embarrassment for a team with Blackpool's pedigree. Finishing in seventh position, Blackpool took on and defeated Hartlepool in the Play-Off semi-finals before meeting Leyton Orient at the Millennium Stadium for the privilege of playing in next season's Second Division. A dramatic game saw the Seasiders ultimately triumph 4-2, thus restoring Second Division football to Bloomfield Road after a gap of one year. However, fate has not been kind to promoted teams in recent years and the club will struggle to retain its new found status in 2001/02.

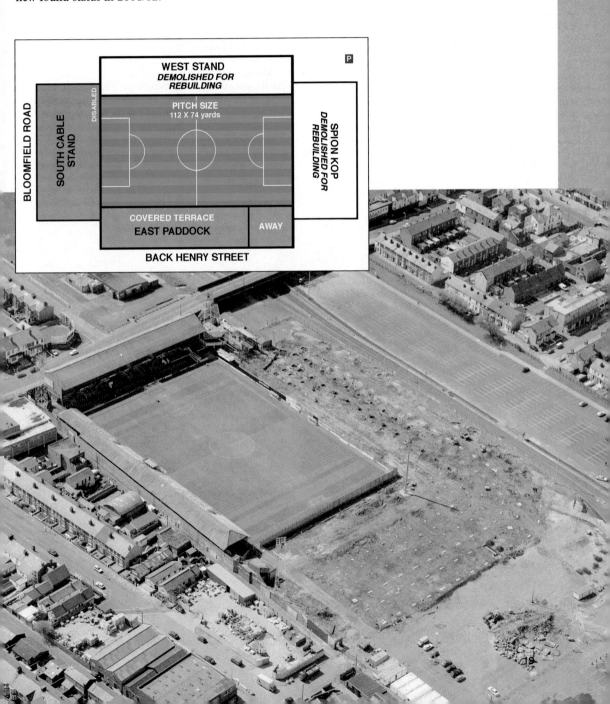

BOLTON WANDERERS

Reebok Stadium, Burnden Way, Lostock, Bolton, BL6 6JW

Tel No: 01204 673673
Advance Tickets Tel No: 01204 673601
Fax: 01204 673773
E-Mail: admin@bwfc.co.uk
Web Site: www.boltonfc.co.uk
League: FA Premiership
Brief History: Founded 1874 as Christ Church; name changed 1877. Former grounds: Several Fields, Pikes Lane (1880-95) and Burnden Park (1895-1997). Moved to Reebok Stadium for 1997/98 season. Record attendance (Burnden Park): 69,912. Record attendance of 25,000 at Reebok Stadium first achieved on 20 September 1997
(Total) Current Capacity: 27,800 (all-seater)
Visiting Supporters' Allocation: 5,200 (South Stand)

Club Colours: White shirts, blue shorts
Nearest Railway Station: Horwich Parkway
Parking (Car): 2,000 places at ground with up to 3,000 others in proximity
Parking (Coach/Bus): As directed
Police Force and Tel No: Greater Manchester (01204 522466)
Disabled Visitors' Facilities:
 Wheelchairs: c150 places around the ground
 Blind: Commentary available
Anticipated Developments(s): The station at Horwich Parkway has now opened. There are currently no further plans for the development of the Reebok Stadium.

KEY

↑ North direction (approx)

❶ Junction 6 of M61
❷ A6027 Horwich link road
❸ South Stand (away)
❹ North Stand
❺ Nat Lofthouse Stand
❻ West Stand
❼ M61 northbound to M6 and Preston (at J6)
❽ M61 southbound to Manchester (at J6)
❾ To Horwich and Bolton
❿ To Lostock Junction BR station
⓫ Horwich Parkway station

Above: 688307; Right: 688303

It was third time lucky for Bolton Wanderers and the Play-Offs as the team defeated Preston North End 3-0 in the final at the Millennium Stadium to bring Premiership football back to the Reebok Stadium. In a neck-and-neck race with Blackburn Rovers for most of the season to grab the second automatic promotion spot, Wanderers finished well ahead of the competition in third place. Victory over West Brom in the semi-final set up the Cardiff showdown with local rivals Preston. Whilst there will be undoubted joy in Bolton at the team's elevation, it will be tempered by the reality of the fact that Bolton has struggled at the higher level on its previous acquaintance with the Premiership and, over recent years, those teams that have been promoted through the Play-Offs — Watford and Manchester City — have been relegated straightaway. No doubt Wanderers will be one of the pre-season favourites for the drop but Sam Allardyce and his team will, no doubt, be hoping to prove the pundits wrong and emulate Ipswich Town rather than Manchester City.

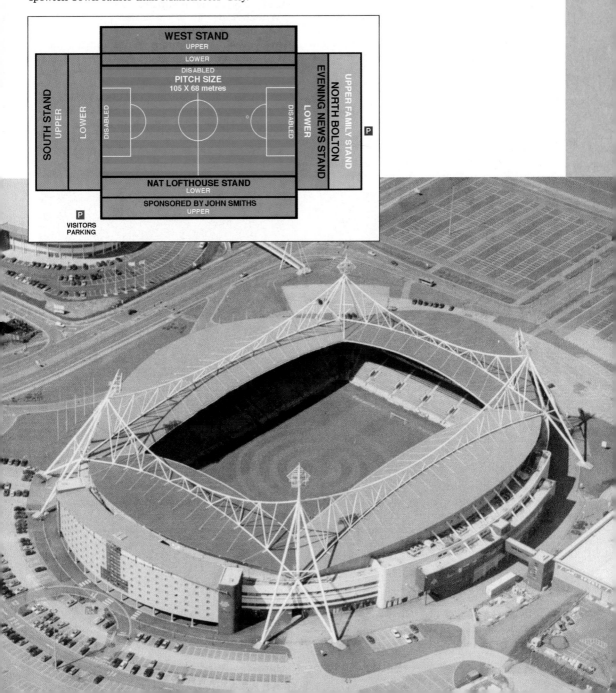

A.F.C. BOURNEMOUTH

Dean Court, Bournemouth, Dorset, BH7 7AF

Tel No: 01202 395381
Advance Tickets Tel No: 01202 397939
Fax: 01202 309797
E-Mail: enquiries@afcb.co.uk
Web Site: www.afcb.co.uk
League: 2nd Division
Brief History: Founded 1890 as Boscombe St. John's, changed to Boscombe (1899), Bournemouth & Boscombe Athletic (1923) and A.F.C. Bournemouth (1971). Former grounds Kings Park (twice) and Castlemain Road, Pokesdown. Moved to Dean Court in 1910. Record attendance 28,799
(Total) Current Capacity: 10,770 (3,141 seated) (prior to redevelopment)
Visiting Supporters' Allocation: To be confirmed
Club Colours: Red and black shirts, black shorts
Nearest Railway Station: Bournemouth

Parking (Car): Large car park adjacent ground
Parking (Coach/Bus): Large car park adjacent ground
Police Force and Tel No: Dorset (01202 552099)
Disabled Visitors' Facilities:
Wheelchairs: To be confirmed
Blind: No special facility
Anticipated Development(s): Although it was thought that the club would seek to relocate, in the event the decision was taken to redevelop at Dean Court. Work started towards the end of the 2000/01 season and will involve the pitch being rotated by 90°. The new Dean Court is scheduled to open with the start of the 2001/02 season, although the club has obtained permission to play early home games at Dorchester if necessary.

KEY

C Club Offices
S Club Shop
E Entrance(s) for visiting supporters
R Refreshment bars for visiting supporters
T Toilets for visiting supporters

⬆ North direction (approx)

❶ Car Park
❷ A338 Wessex Way
❸ To Bournemouth BR Station (1½ miles)
❹ To A31 & M27
❺ Thistlebarrow Road
❻ King's Park Drive
❼ Littledown Avenue
❽ A3049 Ashley Road

Above: 688899; Right: 688889

A promising season for Mel Machin's Bournemouth in their last campaign at the 'old' Dean Court saw the Cherries improve dramatically on the 16th position achieved at the end of 1999/2000. In the event, it was the results on the last day of the season that conspired to ensure that Bournemouth finished seventh — and thus out of the Play-Offs — being pipped at the end by ambitious Wigan Athletic. Both teams drew — Wigan 0-0 at home to Bristol City and Bournemouth 3-3 at Reading, where an 88th minute equaliser by the home team deprived Bournemouth of the victory that would have ensure the team a place in the Play-Offs. Thus the new Dean Court will see Second Division football in 2001/02; however, if the team continues to improve as much as it did in 2000/01, a serious push for automatic promotion ought to be a possibility.

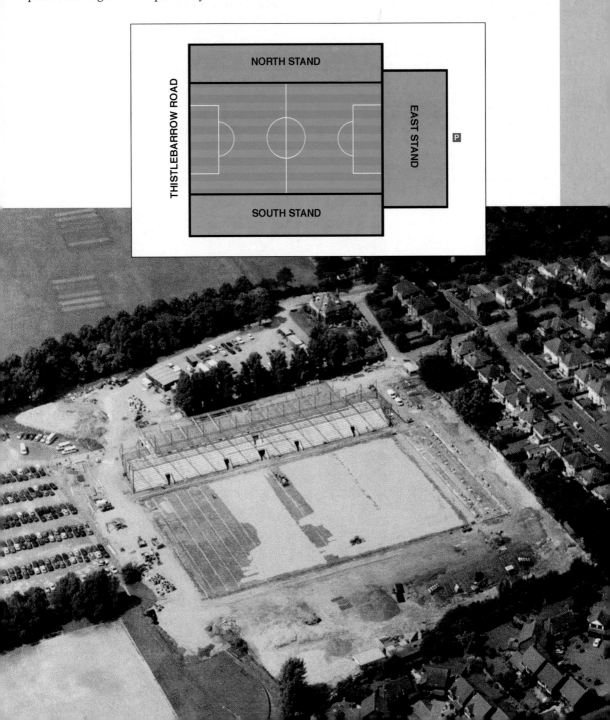

BRADFORD CITY

Bradford & Bingley Stadium, Valley Parade, Bradford, BD8 7DY

Tel No: 01274 773355
Advance Tickets Tel No: 01274 770022
Fax: 01274 773356
Web Site: www.bradfordcityfc.co.uk
E-Mail: bradfordcityfc@compuserve.com
League: 1st Division
Brief History: Founded 1903 (formerly Manningham Northern Union Rugby Club founded in 1876). Continued use of Valley Parade, joined 2nd Division on re-formation. Record attendance: 39,146
(Total) Current Capacity: 25,000 (all seated)
Visiting Supporters' Allocation: 1,842 (all seated) in Symphony stand
Club Colours: Claret and amber shirts, black shorts
Nearest Railway Station: Bradford Forster Square
Parking (Car): Street parking and car parks
Parking (Coach/Bus): As directed by Police
Police Force and Tel No: West Yorkshire (01274 723422)

Disabled Visitors' Facilities:
Wheelchairs: 110 places in Sunwin, CIBA and Carlsberg stands
Blind: Commentary available
Anticipated Development(s): Work on the construction of the new northwest Corner Stand and the second tier of the main Sunwin Stand progressed during the 2000/01 season, although original plans to have the latter completed by February proved to be optimistic. The second tier was completed towards the end of the season. The club has plans for the construction of the remainder of the Sunwin Stand, but this work requires consent to close a road, and also for the building of a second tier on the Midland Road (Ciba) Stand with a view to increasing capacity to 30,000. In terms of time scale, much will depend on the club regaining Premiership status.

KEY

C Club Offices
S Club Shop
E Entrance(s) for visiting supporters
R Refreshment bars for visiting supporters
T Toilets for visiting supporters

↑ North direction (approx)

❶ Midland Road
❷ Valley Parade
❸ A650 Manningham Lane
❹ To City Centre, Forster Square and Interchange BR Stations M606 & M62
❺ To Keighley
❻ Car Parks
❼ Sunwin Stand (being rebuilt)
❽ Midland (CIBA) Stand
❾ Symphony Stand
❿ Carlsberg Stand

Above: 688342; Right: 688338

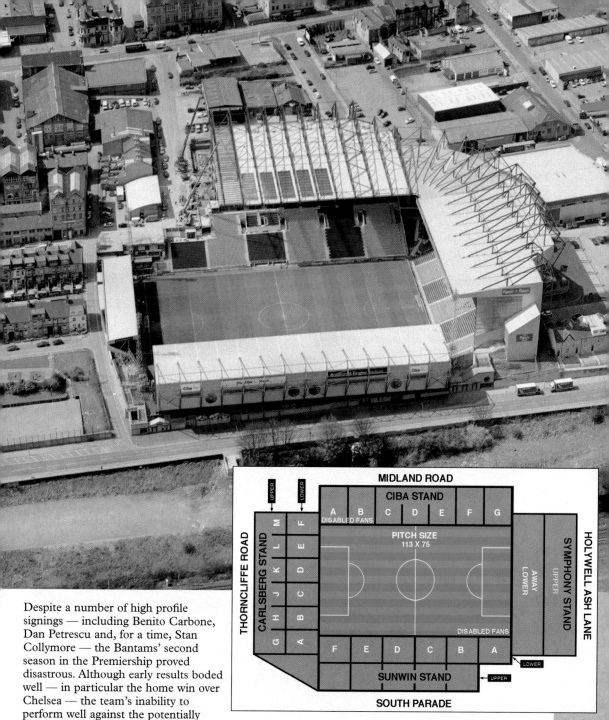

MIDLAND ROAD

CIBA STAND

THORNCLIFFE ROAD

CARLSBERG STAND

UPPER — LOWER

M L K J H G | F E D C B A

A B DISABLED FANS | C D E F G

PITCH SIZE
113 X 75

DISABLED FANS

AWAY LOWER

SYMPHONY STAND

UPPER

HOLYWELL ASH LANE

F E D C B A

LOWER

SUNWIN STAND

UPPER

SOUTH PARADE

Despite a number of high profile signings — including Benito Carbone, Dan Petrescu and, for a time, Stan Collymore — the Bantams' second season in the Premiership proved disastrous. Although early results boded well — in particular the home win over Chelsea — the team's inability to perform well against the potentially weaker teams resulted in the sacking of tyro manager Chris Hutchings and his replacement by ex-Hearts boss Jim Jefferies. Under instructions, given the almost certain relegation of the team, to reduce overheads, the second half of the season saw almost daily departures from Valley Parade, although, as in 1999/2000, the team did string together an impressive set of results towards the end of the season. Unfortunately, this year, it came too late and City will be playing local derbies at Barnsley rather than Leeds in 2001/02. However, with the expansion of Valley Parade and a still ambitious chairman in Geoffrey Richmond, expect the Bantams to feature in the First Division promotion race this season. Much will depend on the squad that Jefferies is able to muster for the season, particularly given Richmond's desire to reduce massively the club's wage bill.

BRENTFORD

Griffin Park, Braemar Road, Brentford, Middlesex, TW8 0NT

Tel No: 020 8847 2511
Advance Tickets Tel No: 020 8847 2511
Fax: 020 8568 9940
Web Site: www.brentfordfc.co.uk
E-Mail: enquiries@brentfordfc.co.uk
League: 2nd Division
Brief History: Founded 1889. Former Grounds: Clifden House Ground, Benn's Field (Little Ealing), Shotters Field, Cross Roads, Boston Park Cricket Ground, moved to Griffin Park in 1904. Founder-members Third Division (1920). Record attendance 38,678
(Total) Current Capacity: 12,750 (8,907 seated)
Visiting Supporters' Allocation: 2,263 (636 seated) in Brook Street Stand
Club Colours: Red and white striped shirts, black shorts
Nearest Railway Station: Brentford, South Ealing (tube)

Parking (Car): Street parking (restricted)
Parking (Coach/Bus): Layton Road car park
Police Force and Tel No: Metropolitan (020 8577 1212)
Disabled Visitors' Facilities:
  Wheelchairs: Braemar Road
  Blind: Commentary available
Anticipated Development(s): There is still talk that the club would like to relocate to a new 15,000-seat stadium at Feltham Arena. This project, however, will cost some £20 million and it is by no means certain that Brentford will make the move. More likely, in the short term, is that the club will vacate Griffin Park and groundshare with either Woking or Kingstonian. Provisional agreement with the former was reached in February 2001 with a view to groundsharing from August 2003. However, nothing is confirmed and expect the Bees to spend at least another season at Griffin Park.

KEY

- **C** Club Offices
- **S** Club Shop
- **E** Entrance(s) for visiting supporters
- **R** Refreshment bars for visiting supporters
- **T** Toilets for visiting supporters

↑ North direction (approx)

❶ Ealing Road
❷ Braemar Road
❸ Brook Road South
❹ To M4 (1/4 mile) & South Ealing Tube Station (1 mile)
❺ Brentford BR Station
❻ To A315 High Street & Kew Bridge

With Ron Noades as chairman and Ray Lewington in charge of coaching, 2000/01 was a season of some success at Griffin Park following the collapse of form during 1999/2000. However, too many important players were allowed to leave during the course of the season to ensure an effective march towards the Play-Offs and too many league points were thrown away in games that could have been won. A 14th place was an improvement on the 17th achieved in 1999/2000, but only just, and the season was brought to life by the team reaching the final of the LDV Vans trophy, held at the Millennium Stadium in Cardiff. Unfortunately defeat by Port Vale ensured that the Bees ended up without the silverware, but the cup run will give fans some optimism for 2001/02, particularly with Steve Coppell now reunited with Ron Noades — the old Crystal Palace partnership — following Lewington's departure to Watford.

BRIGHTON & HOVE ALBION

Withdean Stadium, Tongdean Lane, Brighton BN1 5JD

Tel No: 01273 778855
Fax: 01273 321095
Advance Ticket Tel No: 01273 776992
Web Site: www.seagulls.co.uk
E-Mail: seagulls@bhafc.co.uk
League: 2nd Division
Brief History: Founded 1900 as Brighton & Hove Rangers, changed to Brighton & Hove Albion 1902. Former grounds: Home Farm (Withdean), County Ground, Goldstone Ground (1902-1997), Priestfield Stadium (ground share with Gillingham) 1997-1999; moved to Withdean Stadium 1999. Founder members of the 3rd Division 1920. Record attendance (at Goldstone Ground): 36,747.
(Total) Current Capacity: c7,000
Visiting Supporters' Allocation: 325 (North Stand) (min)
Club Colours: Blue and white striped shirts, blue shorts
Nearest Railway Station: Preston Park
Parking (Cars): Street parking in the immediate vicinity of the ground is residents' only. This will be strictly enforced and it is suggested that intending visitors should use parking facilities away from the ground and use the proposed park and ride bus services that will be provided.
Parking (Coach/Bus): As directed
Police Force and Tel No: Sussex (01273 778922)
Disabled Visitors' Facilities
  Wheelchairs: Facilities in both North and South stands
  Blind: No special facility
Anticipated Development(s): Towards the end of June 2000 it was announced that the club had been granted permission to remain at Withdean for a further two years, up to the end of the 2002/03 season. This potentially coincides quite well with the proposed development of the new stadium at Village Way North, Falmer, which is expected to be completed for the start of the 2003/04 season. The new ground will have a 25,000 all-seated capacity.

KEY
Club Address:
  118 Queen's Road, Brighton, BN1 3XG.
  Tel: 01273 778855
  Fax: 01273 321095

Shop Address:
  6 Queen's Road, Brighton

⬆ North direction (approx)

Note: All games at Withdean will be all-ticket with no cash admissions on the day.

❶ Withdean Stadium
❷ London-Brighton railway line
❸ London Road (A23)
❹ Tongdean Lane
❺ Valley Drive
❻ To Brighton town centre and main railway station (1.75 miles)
❼ Tongdean Lane (with bridge under railway)
❽ South Stand
❾ A23 northwards to Crawley
❿ To Preston Park railway station
⓫ North Stand

28

Above: 684569; Right: 684566

Following a number of years when the Seagulls flirted with demotion to the Nationwide Conference, 2000/01 proved to be a season of triumph for Mickey Adams team, as Brighton clinched promotion back to the Second Division. However, fans would be well advised to expect a torrid time back at this higher level; experience over the past couple of seasons is that promoted teams often struggle to establish themselves and regularly find themselves involved in the relegation battle. Given Adams' success, it is inevitable that both he and star striker Bobby Zamora are being touted as possible departees during the summer. If either does move on, the Seagulls' struggles will be even greater.

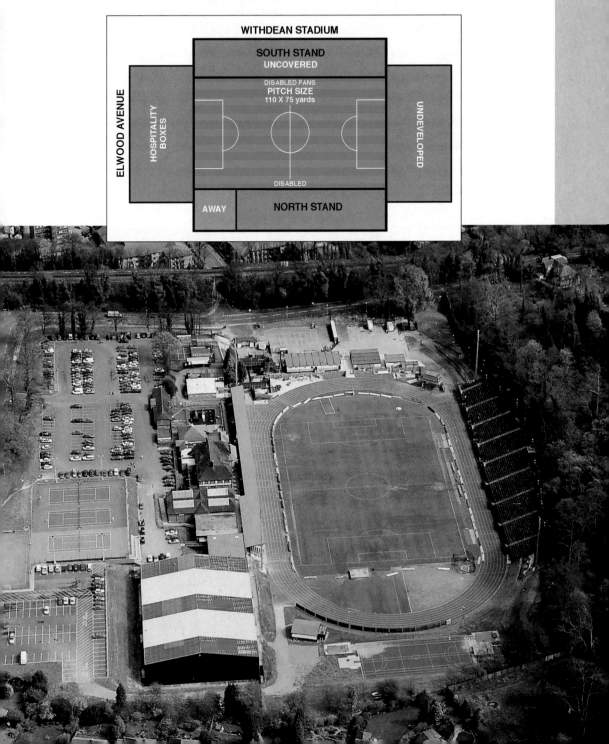

WITHDEAN STADIUM

SOUTH STAND
UNCOVERED

DISABLED FANS
PITCH SIZE
110 X 75 yards

ELWOOD AVENUE

HOSPITALITY
BOXES

UNDEVELOPED

DISABLED

AWAY

NORTH STAND

BRISTOL CITY

Ashton Gate, Winterstoke Road, Ashton Road, Bristol BS3 2JE

Tel No: 0117 963 0630
Advance Tickets Tel No: 0117 966 6666
Fax: 0117 963 0700
Web Site: www.bcfc.co.uk
League: 2nd Division
Brief History: Founded 1894 as Bristol South End changed to Bristol City in 1897. Former Ground: St John's Lane, Bedminster, moved to Ashton Gate in 1904. Record attendance 43,445
(Total) Current Capacity: 21,200 (all seated)
Visiting Supporters' Allocation: 2,500 in Wedlock End (all seated; can be increased to 5,500 if necessary)
Club Colours: Red shirts, red shorts
Nearest Railway Station: Bristol Temple Meads

Parking (Car): Street parking
Parking (Coach/Bus): Marsh Road
Police Force and Tel No: Avon/Somerset (0117 927 7777)
Disabled Visitors' Facilities:
Wheelchairs: Advanced notice not required
Blind: Commentary available
Future Development(s): There are plans for the redevelopment of Ashton Gate, starting off with the construction of a new 12,000-seat stand to replace the existing Brunel Williams Stand. However, there are now also proposals for the construction of a brand new 36,000-seat stadium at Hengrove Park.

KEY

C Club Offices
S Club Shop
E Entrance(s) for visiting supporters

↑ North direction (approx)

❶ A370 Ashton Road
❷ A3209 Winterstoke Road
❸ To Temple Meads Station (1 1/2 miles)
❹ To City Centre, A4, M32 & M4
❺ Database Wedlock Stand
❻ Atyeo Stand

Following the departure of the unpopular Tony Pulis, Danny Wilson, who had had success on a limited budget with Barnsley but who had struggled with Sheffield Wednesday, was the new man in the Ashton Gate hot-seat. City was another team that showed consistency over 1999/2000, finishing again ninth in 2000/01, although the points' differential was reduced from 18 to seven over the season. If Wilson can maintain the team's momentum — in particular in converting some of the team's numerous draws into victories — then City ought to be one of the clubs pushing for one of the automatic promotion spots. Anything lower than a Play-Off place will be considered by most to be a failure.

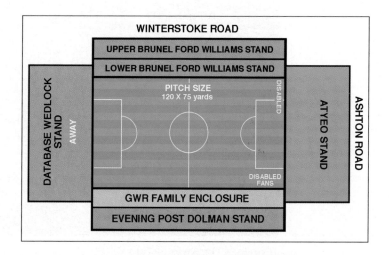

BRISTOL ROVERS

The Memorial Stadium, Filton Avenue, Horfield, Bristol BS7 0AQ

Registered Office: The Beeches, Broomhill Road, Brislington, Bristol BS4 5BF
Tel No: 0117 924 7474
Advance Tickets Tel No: 0117 924 3200
Fax: 0117 924 4454
Web Site: http://www.bristolrovers.co.uk
E-Mail: webmaster@bristolrovers.co.uk
League: 3rd Division
Brief History: Founded 1883 as Black Arabs, changed to Eastville Rovers (1884), Bristol Eastville Rovers (1896) and Bristol Rovers (1897). Former grounds: Purdown, Three Acres, The Downs (Horfield), Ridgeway, Bristol Stadium (Eastville), Twerton Park (1986-96), moved to The Memorial Ground 1996. Record attendance: (Eastville) 38,472, (Twerton Park) 9,813, (Memorial Ground) 9,274
(Total) Current Capacity: 11,917 (4,000 seated); standing capacity of 8,000 includes 500 on the Family Terrace

Visiting Supporters' Allocation: 1,132 (Centenary Stand Terrace)
Club Colours: Blue and white quartered shirts, white shorts
Nearest Railway Station: Filton or Stapleton Road
Parking (Car): Limited parking at ground for home fans only; street parking also available
Parking (Coach/Bus): As directed
Police Force and Tel No: Avon/Somerset (0117 927 7777)
Disabled Visitors' Facilities:
  Wheelchairs: 35 wheelchair positions
  Blind: Limited provision
Anticipated Development(s): Although work has been completed on the temporary structures at the Scoreboard and Terrace ends, the club's intention remains to construct a 20,000 all-seater stadium at the ground in the long term. There are proposals for the construction of a further temporary stand in the southwest corner of the ground.

KEY

C Rugby Club offices
E Entrance(s) for visiting supporters
R Refrshments for visiting supporters
T Toilets for visiting supporters

⬆ North direction (approx)

❶ Filton Avenue
❷ Gloucester Road
❸ Muller Road
❹ To Bristol city centre (2.5 miles) and BR Temple Meads station (3 miles)
❺ Downer Road
❻ Car Park
❼ To M32 J2 (1.5 miles)
❽ Strathmore Road
❾ To Filton (1.5 miles)
❿ Centenary Stand
⓫ West Stand

Above: 684922; *Right:* 684914

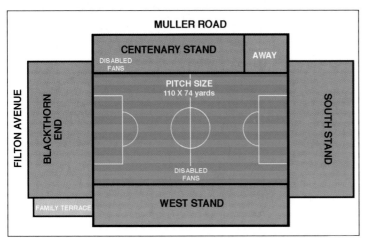

MULLER ROAD

CENTENARY STAND

DISABLED FANS

AWAY

FILTON AVENUE

BLACKTHORN END

PITCH SIZE
110 X 74 yards

DISABLED FANS

SOUTH STAND

FAMILY TERRACE

WEST STAND

After a couple of seasons when Rovers seemed destined for higher things, events on the field certainly went pear shaped for Ian Holloway and the team in 2000/01. Poor results led to Holloway's departure in January, but his successor Garry Thompson (as caretaker manager) was unable to reverse the team's fortunes and relegation to the Third Division was confirmed after the penultimate game of the season, despite an impressive 4-0 victory over Wrexham in the final game. Rovers will be fancied to make an immediate return to the Second Division at the end of 2001/02.

BURNLEY

Turf Moor, Harry Potts Way, Burnley, Lancs, BB10 4BX

Tel No: 01282 700000
Advance Tickets Tel No: 01282 700010
Fax: 01282 700014
Web Site: www.burnleyfootballclub.com
E-Mail: info@burnleyfootballclub.net
League: 2nd Division
Brief History: Founded 1882, Burnley Rovers (Rugby Club) combined with another Rugby Club, changed to soccer and name to Burnley. Moved from Calder Vale to Turf Moor in 1882. Founder-members Football League (1888). Record attendance 54,775
(Total) Current Capacity: 22,524 (all seated)
Visiting Supporters' Allocation: 4,125 (all seated in Cricket Field Stand)
Club Colours: Claret with blue sleeved shirts, white with claret and blue trim shorts
Nearest Railway Station: Burnley Central
Parking (Car): Church Street and Fulledge Rec.

(car parks)
Parking (Coach/Bus): As directed by Police
Police Force and Tel No: Lancashire (01282 425001)
Disabled Visitors' Facilities:
  Wheelchairs: Places available in North, East and Cricket Field stands
  Blind: Headsets provided with commentary
Anticipated Development(s): In conjunction with the adjacent Cricket Club, Burnley is proposing a redevelopment of the Cricket Field Stand, which would then be reallocated to home supporters. This would be followed, probably, by a redevelopment of the Bob Lord Stand with the intention of raising the ground's capacity significantly above the current 22,524. There is, however, no schedule for this work, much of which depends upon the financial position of the Cricket Club.

KEY

- **C** Club Offices
- **S** Club Shop
- **E** Entrance(s) for visiting supporters

↑ North direction (approx)

- ❶ Brunshaw Road
- ❷ Belvedere Road
- ❸ Burnley Central BR Station (1/2 mile)
- ❹ Cricket Ground
- ❺ Cricket Field Stand
- ❻ East (Jimmy McIlroy) Stand
- ❼ Bob Lord Stand
- ❽ North (James Hargreaves) Stand

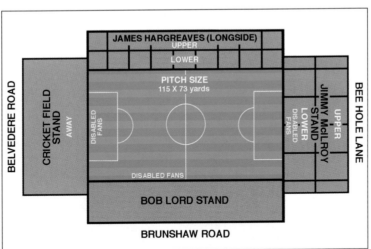

A season of some promise for the Clarets' first campaign back in the First Division saw Stan Ternent's team threatening for a Play-Off position for much of the year, although ultimately missing out. The new season will be viewed with some optimism by the Turf Moor faithful even if the local rivalry with Blackburn will be off the agenda for at least one year.

BURY

Gigg Lane, Bury, Lancashire, BL9 9HR

Tel No: 0161 764 4881
Advance Tickets Tel No: 0161 705 2144
Fax: 0161 764 5521
Web Site: www.buryfc.co.uk
E-Mail: commerce@buryfc.co.uk
League: 2nd Division
Brief History: Founded 1885, no former names or former grounds. Record attendance 35,000
(Total) Current Capacity: 12,500 (all seated)
Visiting Supporters' Allocation: 2,676 (all seated) in West Stand
Club Colours: White shirts, royal blue shorts
Nearest Railway Station: Bury Interchange

Parking (Car): Street parking
Parking (Coach/Bus): As directed by Police
Police Force and Tel No: Greater Manchester (0161 872 5050)
Disabled Visitors' Facilities:
  Wheelchairs: South Stand (home) and West Stand (away)
  Blind: Commentary available
Anticipated Development(s): The completion of the rebuilt Cemetery End means that current plans for the redevelopment of Gigg Lane have been completed.

KEY

C Club Offices
S Club Shop
E Entrance(s) for visiting supporters

↑ North direction (approx)

❶ Car Park
❷ Gigg Lane
❸ A56 Manchester Road
❹ Town Centre & Bury Interchange (Metrolink) (3/4 mile)
❺ West (Manchester Road) Stand
❻ Cemetery End

Above: 684931; Right: 684926

GIGG LANE

MAIN STAND

PITCH SIZE
112 X 72 yards

MANCHESTER ROAD

WEST STAND
AWAY

CEMETERY END
STAND

DISABLED FANS

DISABLED FANS

SOUTH STAND
MILLIKEN ENCLOSURE

The Shakers' second season back in the Second Division was again marked by a struggle against relegation, although the team failed to fulfil the prophecies of many pundits and actually managed to retain its Second Division status. Finishing 16th was better than seemed possible at one stage when relegation did seem a real possibility but it is doubtful whether the Shakers will be able to offer a sustained challenge for the Play-Offs or promotion in 2001/02.

CAMBRIDGE UNITED

Abbey Stadium, Newmarket Road, Cambridge, CB5 8LN

Tel No: 01223 566500
Advance Tickets Tel No: 01223 566500
Fax: 01223 566502
Web Site: www.cambridgeunited.com
E-mail: andrea@cambridgeunited.net
League: 2nd Division
Brief History: Founded 1913 as Abbey United, changed to Cambridge United in 1951. Former Grounds: Midsummer Common, Stourbridge Common, Station Farm Barnwell (The Celery Trenches) & Parker's Piece, moved to Abbey Stadium in 1933. Record attendance 14,000
(Total) Current Capacity: 9,247 (3,198 seated) (prior to redevelopment)
Visiting Supporters' Allocation: Limited standing in north end of Habbin Stand
Club Colours: Amber and black shirts, amber shorts
Nearest Railway Station: Cambridge (2 miles)
Parking (Car): Coldhams Common

Parking (Coach/Bus): Coldhams Common
Police Force and Tel No: Cambridge (01223 358966)
Disabled Visitors' Facilities:
  Wheelchairs: Limited number that should be pre-booked
  Blind: No special facility
Anticipated Development(s): In December 2000 the Football Foundation gave a grant of £2 million towards the anticipated £4.5 million cost of redeveloping the ground and a director was appointed in January 2001 to oversee the work. Work started on the redevelopment of the ground in the summer of 2001 (unfortunately after the cut-off date for photography in the book) and involves the construction of new South and North stands – the former partially over the allotments – and the shifting of the pitch 15yd to the south. The new stadium will ultimately have a 10,000 all-seated capacity although standing accommodation will be retained as long as League rules permit.

KEY

C Club Offices
S Club Shop
E Entrance(s) for visiting supporters
R Refreshment bars for visiting supporters
T Toilets for visiting supporters

↑ North direction (approx)

❶ A1134 Newmarket Road
❷ To A11 for Newmarket
❸ To City Centre, Cambridge BR Station (2 miles) and M11
❹ Whitehill Road
❺ South Terrace
❻ Habbin Stand
❼ Main Stand
❽ North Terrace

Above: 687753; *Right:* 687744

SOUTH STAND
(UNDER CONSTRUCTION)

AWAY

HABBIN STAND
PARTIALLY COVERED
TERRACE

PITCH SIZE
110 X 74 yards

DISABLED FANS

DISABLED
FANS

NEWMARKET ROAD (A1134)

NORTH STAND
(UNDER CONSTRUCTION)

MAIN STAND

WHITEHALL ROAD

Promoted at the end of end of 1998/99, when the team finished as runners-up to champions Brentford in the Third Division, many expected Cambridge United to maintain their upwardly mobile lifestyle and threaten the promotion places in Division Two. In the event, Roy McFarland's team was involved in a desperate struggle in 1999/2000, but at the wrong end of the table. In the relegation zone for much of the season, the team was eventually to finish four points and two places above the drop, despite a last day defeat at home by Wycombe Wanderers.

CARDIFF CITY

Ninian Park, Sloper Road, Cardiff, CF11 8SX

Tel No: 029 2022 1001
Advance Tickets Tel No: 029 2022 2858
Fax: 029 2034 1148
Web Site: www.cardiffcity.fc.co.uk
E-mail: webmaker@ccafc.com
League: 2nd Division
Brief History: Founded 1899. Former Grounds: Riverside Cricket Club, Roath, Sophia Gardens, Cardiff Arms Park and The Harlequins Rugby Ground, moved to Ninian Park in 1910. Ground record attendance 61,566 (Wales v. England, 1961)
(Total) Current Capacity: 16,047 (12,647 seated)
Visiting Supporters' Allocation: 4,478 (1,078 seated in Grandstand Blocks A-B; 3,400 in Grangetown Terrace)

Club Colours: Blue shirts, white shorts
Nearest Railway Station: Ninian Park (adjacent) (Cardiff Central 1 mile)
Parking (Car): Opposite Ground, no street parking around ground
Parking (Coach/Bus): Sloper Road
Police Force and Tel No: South Wales (029 2022 2111)
Disabled Visitors' Facilities:
  Wheelchairs: Corner Canton Stand/Popular Bank (covered)
  Blind: No special facility
Anticipated Development(s): Now under the ownership of the ebullient Sam Hammam, the club has announced plans for relocation although these are still tentative.

KEY

C Club Offices
S Club Shop
E Entrance(s) for visiting supporters
R Refreshment bars for visiting supporters
T Toilets for visiting supporters (Terrace only, when used)

↑ North direction (approx)

❶ Sloper Road
❷ B4267 Leckwith Road
❸ Car Park
❹ To A4232 & M4 Junction 33 (8 miles)
❺ Ninian Park Road
❻ To City Centre & Cardiff Central BR Station (1 mile)
❼ To A48 Western Avenue, A49M, and M4 Junction 32 and 29
❽ Ninian Park BR station

Above: 688007; *Right:* 688023

City's yo-yo existence between the Third and Second Division continued, with a further successful promotion campaign. There will be much local pride in the fact that one of the teams Cardiff is replacing is rival Swansea City. With former Wimbledon owner Sam Hammam now established as chairman, the new supremo seems determined to try to recreate the same 'Crazy Gang' ethos that marked much of his time in south London. Whether this will be enough to keep City in the Second Division — given the team's immediate relegation last time — only time will tell; one thing is certain, however, and that life is going to be interesting at Ninian Park.

CARLISLE UNITED

Brunton Park, Warwick Road, Carlisle, CA1 1LL

Tel No: 01228 526237
Advance Tickets Tel No: 01228 526237
Fax: 01228 530138
Website: www.carlisleunited.co.uk
E-Mail: admin@carlisleunited.co.uk
League: 3rd Division
Brief History: Founded 1904 as Carlisle United (previously named Shaddongate United). Former Grounds: Millholme Bank and Devonshire Park, moved to Brunton Park in 1909. Record attendance 27,500
(Total) Current Capacity: 16,500 (7,209 seated)
Visiting Supporters' Allocation: 2,000 (East Stand blocks 1 to 4)

Club Colours: Royal blue shirts, blue shorts
Nearest Railway Station: Carlisle Citadel
Parking (Car): Rear of ground
Parking (Coach/Bus): St Aiden's Road car park
Police Force and Tel No: Cumbria (01228 28191)
Disabled Visitors' Facilities:
  Wheelchairs: East Stand and Paddock (prior arrangement)
  Blind: No special facilities
Anticipated Development(s): Long term plans for a 28,000 all-seater stadium, but nothing concrete planned after completion of the new East Stand.

KEY
- **C** Club Offices
- **E** Entrance(s) for visiting supporters
- **R** Refreshment bars for visiting supporters
- **T** Toilets for visiting supporters

↑ North direction (approx)

- ❶ A69 Warwick Road
- ❷ To M6 Junction 43
- ❸ Carlisle Citadel BR Station (1 mile)
- ❹ Greystone Road
- ❺ Car Park
- ❻ Petteril End (closed)

Another season, another dogfight to avoid the drop to the Conference and yet, once again, Carlisle United survive to battle once more in the Third Division. It is to be supposed that United fans will regard the fact that the team had already guaranteed League football in 2001/02 before the last day of the season as being a considerable advance on the previous two years when the club needed results to go its way on both occasions in order to ensure League survival. It is difficult to anticipate 2001/02 being anything other than another battle to avoid the fate of Chester City, Scarborough, Doncaster Rovers and Hereford United — long-established League clubs that have failed to hold onto that status and then struggled in the Conference.

CHARLTON ATHLETIC

The Valley, Floyd Road, Charlton, London, SE7 8BL

Tel No: 020 833 4000
Advance Tickets Tel No: 020 8333 4010
Fax: 020 8333 4001
Web Site: http://www.cafc.co.uk
E-Mail: contact@cafc.co.uk
League: FA Premier
Brief History: Founded 1905. Former grounds: Siemens Meadows, Woolwich Common, Pound Park, Angerstein Athletic Ground, The Mount Catford, Selhurst Park (Crystal Palace FC), Boleyn Ground (West Ham United FC), The Valley (1912-23, 1924-85, 1992-date). Founder Members 3rd Division South. Record attendance 75,031
(Total) Current Capacity: 26,000 (all seated)
Visiting Supporters' Allocation: 2,000 (all seated in South Stand)

Club Colours: Red shirts, white shorts
Nearest Railway Station: Charlton
Parking (Car): Street parking
Parking (Coach/Bus): As directed by Police
Police Force and Tel No: Metropolitan (020 8853 8212)
Disabled Visitors' Facilities:
  Wheelchairs: East/West/South stands
  Blind: Commentary, 12 spaces
Anticipated Development(s): Work started on the construction of the new £9 million 6,500-seat North Stand in March 2001, with the intention of raising the ground's capacity to 26,000 by the start of the new season. Further work will eventually see the capacity increased to almost 30,000.

KEY

E Entrance(s) for visiting supporters

R Refreshment bars for visiting supporters

T Toilets for visiting supporters

↑ North Direction (approx)

❶ Harvey Gardens
❷ A206 Woolwich Road
❸ Valley Grove
❹ Floyd Road
❺ Charlton BR Station
❻ East Stand
❼ North Stand (being rebuilt)
❽ West stand
❾ South stand (away)
❿ Charlton Church Lane
⓫ Charlton Lane

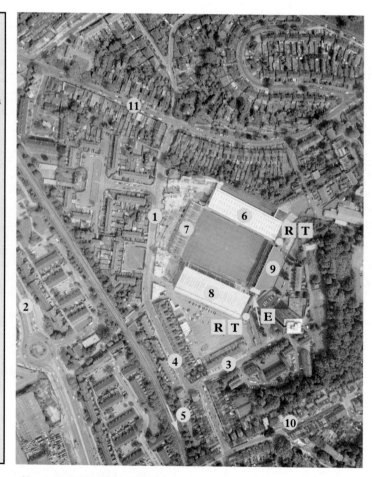

Above: 688371; *Right:* 688363

Widely regarded as perhaps the best equipped of the three promoted teams to retain Premiership status, Charlton's successes have, to a significant extent, been overshadowed by the exploits of Ipswich Town. However, at the start of the season, if fans had been asked if they would have settled for a top-half finish, the realists would have been delighted. Aided by strong home form, Athletic proved that the sabbatical year in the First Division had prepared them well for renewed acquaintance with the Premiership, and the results showed the justification of the club in retaining the services of Alan Curbishley and of the bulk of the squad. Judicious additions to the squad during the season assisted the club's survival and fans can look forward to another season of solid mid-table safety in 2001/02.

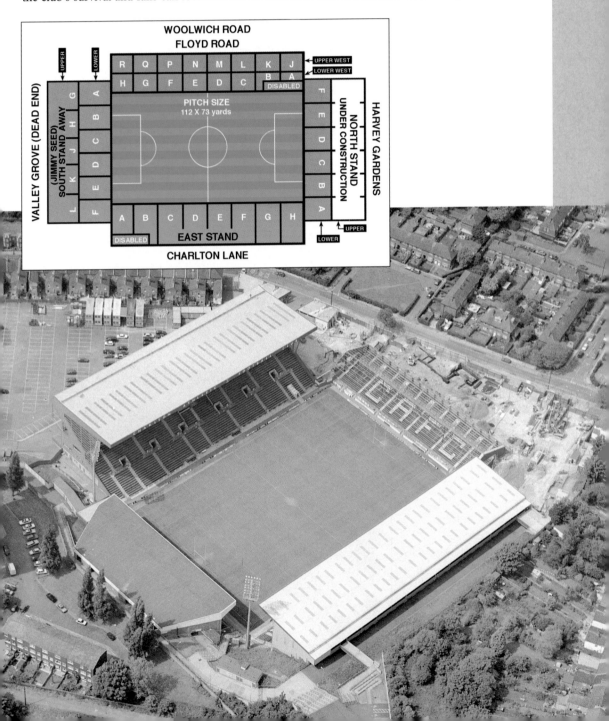

CHELSEA

Stamford Bridge, Fulham Road, London, SW6 1HS

Tel No: 020 7385 5545
Advance Tickets Tel No: 020 7386 7799
Fax: 020 7381 4831
Web Site: www.chelseafc.co.uk
League: F.A. Premier
Brief History: Founded 1905. Admitted to Football League (2nd Division) on formation. Stamford Bridge venue for F.A. Cup Finals 1919-22. Record attendance 82,905
(Total) Current Capacity: 42,500 (all seated)
Visiting Supporters' Allocation: Approx. 1,600 (East Stand Lower; can be increased to 3,200 if required)
Club Colours: Blue shirts, blue shorts

Nearest Railway Station: Fulham Broadway or West Brompton
Parking (Car): Street parking
Parking (Coach/Bus): As directed by Police
Police Force and Tel No: Metropolitan (020 7385 1212)
Disabled Visitors' Facilities:
  Wheelchairs: East Stand
  Blind: No special facility
Anticipated Development(s): With the long awaited completion of the second tier of the West Stand now achieved, redevelopment of Stamford Bridge as a stadium is now complete.

KEY

⬆ North direction (approx)

❶ A308 Fulham Road
❷ Central London
❸ To Fulham Broadway Tube Station
❹ Mathew Harding Stand
❺ East Stand
❻ West Stand
❼ South (Shed) Stand
❽ West Brompton Station

Above: 688355; *Right:* 688356

Following a disappointing start to the season (particularly for a club expected to be challenging for the championship), including a 2-0 defeat away at Bradford City and a first round defeat by an unfancied Swiss team in the UEFA Cup, it still came as a shock when Gianluca Vialli was shown the door at Stamford Bridge. In a further surprise, his successor was fellow Italian Claudio Ranieri and, initially, it appeared that Ken Bates's acumen had let him down. In the event, Chelsea's home form improved immeasurably and by the end of the season enough points had been gathered to ensure a further tilt at the UEFA Cup in 2001/02. With the squad likely to face some rebuilding during the summer, Chelsea ought to be one of the fancied teams to challenge Manchester United for the championship in the new campaign, but the team will have to ensure that it doesn't come a cropper against the Premiership's perceived whipping boys.

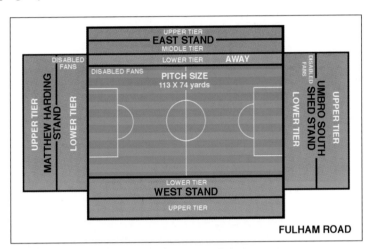

CHELTENHAM TOWN

Whaddon Road, Cheltenham, Gloucestershire GL52 5NA

Tel No: 01242 573558
Advance Tickets Tel No: 01242 573558
Fax: 01242 224675
Web Site: www.the-robins.com
E-Mail: office@cheltenhamtownfc.com
League: 3rd Divison
Brief History: Cheltenham Town was founded in 1892. It moved to Whaddon Road in 1932 having previously played at Carter's Field. After two seasons in the Conference it achieved Nationwide League status at the end of the 1998/99 season. Record attendance 8,326
(Total) Current Capacity: 6,114 (1,088 seated)
Visiting Supporters' Allocation: 1,470 (maximum comprising 720 in Whaddon Road Terrace – uncovered – and 750 in Wymans Road Stand
Club Colours: Red and white striped shirts, red shorts
Nearest Railway Station: Cheltenham (1.5 miles)

Parking (Car): Limited parking at ground; otherwise on-street
Parking (Coach/Bus): As directed by Police
Police Force and Tel No: Gloucestershire (01242 521321)
Disabled Visitors' Facilities:
  Wheelchairs: Six spaces in front of Main Stand
  Blind: No special facility
Anticipated Development(s): The new Cheltenham & Gloucester Stand opened at the Prestbury End at the start of the 2000/01 season. With this completed, attention will now turn to the Wymans Road side, where a new 2,000-seat stand will be constructed to replace the existing covered terrace. Work on the c£1 million project is due to start in the close season and the new stand should be available during the early part of the new season and will take the ground's capacity to 7,200.

KEY

C Club Offices
E Entrance(s) for visiting supporters

↑ North direction (approx)

❶ B4632 Prestbury Road
❷ Cromwell Road
❸ Whaddon Road
❹ Wymans Road
❺ To B4075 Priors Road
❻ To B4075 Prior Road
❼ To Cheltenham town centre and railway station (1.5 and 2 miles respectively)
❽ Main Stand
❾ Wymans Road Stand
❿ Prestbury Road End
⓫ Whaddon Road End

Above: 688383; *Right:* 688378

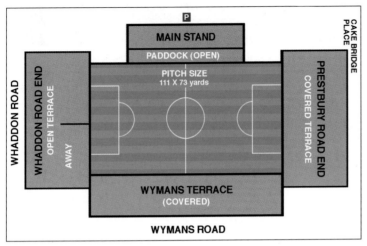

P

MAIN STAND

PADDOCK (OPEN)

PITCH SIZE
111 X 73 yards

WHADDON ROAD

WHADDON ROAD END
OPEN TERRACE

AWAY

PRESTBURY ROAD END
COVERED TERRACE

CAKE BRIDGE PLACE

WYMANS TERRACE
(COVERED)

WYMANS ROAD

The Robins' second season in the Nationwide League again saw the team challenging for one of the Play-Off positions. Unfortunately, results towards the end of the season saw the team once more miss out on the Play-Offs — with a ninth position finish. Perhaps the team's third season in the League will prove more successful for Steve Cotterill's outfit?

CHESTERFIELD

Recreation Ground, Saltergate, Chesterfield, S40 4SX

Tel No: 01246 209765
Advance Tickets Tel No: 01246 209765
Fax: 01246 556799
Web Site: www.chesterfield-fc.co.uk
League: 2nd Division
Brief History: Found 1886. Former Ground: Spital Vale. Formerly named Chesterfield Town. Record attendance 30,968
(Total) Current Capacity: 8,960 (2,674 seated)
Visiting Supporters' Allocation: 2,528 (458 seated)
Club Colours: Blue shirts, blue shorts
Nearest Railway Station: Chesterfield
Parking (Car): Saltergate car park, street parking
Parking (Coach/Bus): As directed by Police

Police Force and Tel No: Derbyshire (01246 220100)
Disabled Visitors' Facilities:
  Wheelchairs: Saltergate Stand
  Blind: No special facility
Anticipated Development(s): The position of Saltergate becomes increasingly tenuous. At one stage during the course of the season the ground's capacity was threatened with a reduction to 2,600 as the Football Licensing Authority rejected the club's appeal to keep the terracing open. However, planning permission was granted on 21 May 2001 for the reconstruction of Saltergate as a 10,000-capacity all-seater stadium. Despite this, progress cannot take place until the club's future viability is assured through the courts.

KEY

C Club Offices
S Club Shop
E Entrance(s) for visiting supporters
R Refreshment bars for visiting supporters
T Toilets for visiting supporters

↑ North direction (approx)

❶ Saltergate
❷ Cross Street
❸ St Margaret's Drive
❹ West Bars
❺ To A617 & M1 Junction 29
❻ To station and town centre

Above: 687948; *Right:* 687940

A strange season for the Spireites where success on the field was mirrored by increasing problems with facilities at Saltergate, by accusations of improper conduct (which resulted in the League docking nine points from the club's total) and a deterioration in the club's financial position. Runaway leaders of the Third Division for most of the campaign, it looked almost guaranteed that Chesterfield would return to the Second Division in triumph after only season in the Third; unfortunately, however, Nicky Law's successful strategy on the field was matched by problems elsewhere in the club and it required a last-day victory over Halifax to keep the team in third place and thus (theoretically — there were

mutterings from Barnet and other Third Division teams over the leniency of the penalty) bring Second Division football to Saltergate in 2001/02. Given the problems that the club is suffering from off the field, it will be nothing short of miraculous if the 2001/02 campaign is anything other than a hard struggle against the drop.

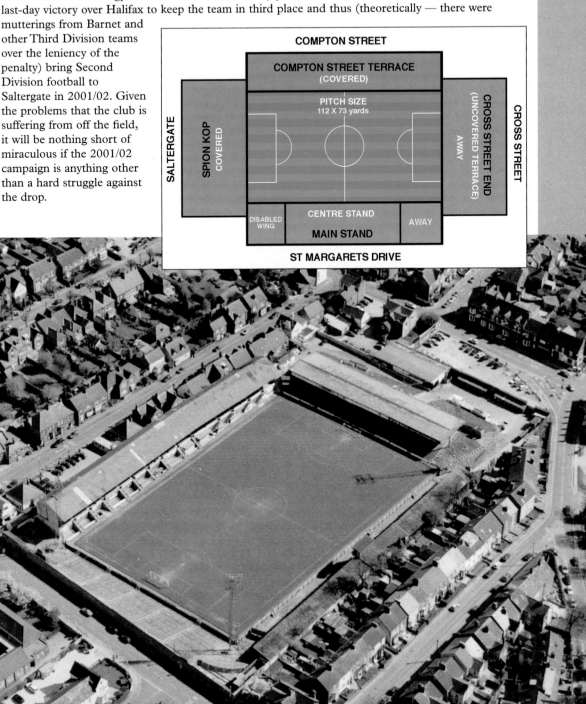

COLCHESTER UNITED

Layer Road Ground, Colchester, CO2 7JJ

Tel No: 01206 508800
Advance Tickets Tel No: 01206 508802
Fax: 01206 508803
Web Site: www.colchesterunited.net
League: 2nd Division
Brief History: Founded 1937, joined Football League 1950, relegated 1990, promoted 1992. Record attendance 19,072
(Total) Current Capacity: 7,556 (1,877 seated)
Visiting Supporters' Allocation: 1,342
Club Colours: Royal blue and white shirts, blue shorts
Nearest Railway Station: Colchester Town
Parking (Car): Street parking
Parking (Coach/Bus): Boadicea Way
Police Force and Tel No: Essex (01206 762212)

Disabled Visitors' Facilities:
  Wheelchairs: Space for six in front of terrace (next to Main Stand)
  Blind: Space for 3 blind persons and 3 guides (two regularly occupied by home supporters)
Anticipated Development(s): In early 1998 the club, in conjunction with the local council, undertook a feasibility study into whether it was feasible to develop Layer Road or whether a new stadium should be built. Consultants in early 1999 suggested the construction of a new 10,000-seat stadium, possibly at Stanhope. Towards the end of the 2000-01 season plans for the new ground – including an artist's impression, were released, although no time-scale was confirmed. Expect United to remain at Layer Road for at least another season.

KEY

C Club Offices
S Club Shop
E Entrance(s) for visiting supporters
R Refreshment bars for visiting supporters
T Toilets for visiting supporters

↑ North direction (approx)

❶ B1026 Layer Road
❷ Town Centre & Colchester Town BR Station (2 miles)
❸ Main Stand
❹ Popular Side
❺ Clock Street End

Despite dispensing with the unpopular Mick Wadsworth during the course of the previous season, 2000/01 was not a great triumph at Layer Road as new manager Steve Whitton found that the squad continued to disappear, with — amongst others — the exotically named Lomana Tresot Lua Lua being transferred away. Tipped as almost relegation certainties by the pundits, the team was certainly vying for that honour for much of the season, although ultimately finishing 17th was a better result than many feared. Another season of Second Division fare beckons at Layer Road, but it may well be that a further season of battling against relegation is also on the cards.

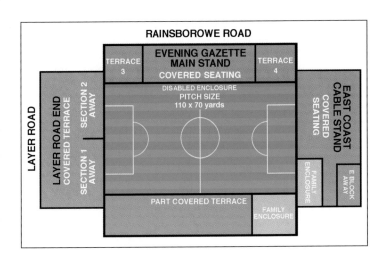

COVENTRY CITY

Highfield Stadium, King Richard Street, Coventry CV2 4FW

Tel No: 02476 234000
Advance Tickets Tel No: 02476 234020
Fax: 02476 234099
Web Site: www.ccfc.co.uk
E-Mail: info@ccfc.co.uk
League: 1st Division
Brief History: Founded 1883 as Singers F.C., changed name to Coventry City in 1898. Former grounds: Dowell's Field, Stoke Road Ground, moved to Highfield Road in 1899. Record attendance 51,455
(Total) Current Capacity: 23,673 all seated
Visiting Supporters' Allocation: 4,148 all seated in Mitchells & Butler Stand
Club Colours: Sky blue and white stripe shirts, white and sky blue shorts

Nearest Railway Station: Coventry
Parking (Car): Street parking
Parking (Coach/Bus): Gosford Green Coach Park
Police Force and Tel No: West Midlands (02476 539010)
Disabled Visitors' Facilities:
Wheelchairs: Clock Stand and East Stand
Blind: Clock Stand (booking necessary)
Anticipated Development(s): Despite the expenditure on Highfield Road in recent years, the club has announced that it intends to build a new 40,000-seat stadium at Foleshill. As yet there is no definite time scale for the proposed move but opening is planned for the start of the 2003/04 season.

KEY

C Club Offices
S Club Shop
E Entrance(s) for visiting supporters
R Refreshment bars for visiting supporters
T Toilets for visiting supporters

⬆ North direction (approx)

❶ Swan Lane
❷ Thackhall Street
❸ Nicholls Street
❹ Catherine Street
❺ A444 Phoenix Way
❻ Heath Road
❼ To M6 Junction 3
❽ To A428 Binley Road
❾ To Gosford Green coach park
❿ To Coventry station (one mile)
⑪ M&B Stand

Above: 688720; *Right:* 688710

After 34 years in the top flight of English football and numerous last days escapes, fate finally caught up with Gordon Strachan's Coventry City with relegation down to the First Division being confirmed by a 3-2 defeat away at neighbours Aston Villa. In a game that City needed to win, all boded well as the team took a 2-0 half-time lead but three goals in the second half gave Villa an unlikely triumph and consigned the Sky Blues to the drop. In truth, relegation comes from results through the whole season and, whilst City always seemed to be playing reasonably well, the club's home form — on which traditionally they have tended to rely — let them down, with too many defeats. Life in the First Division — despite the Premiership 'parachute' — will come as a shock and much will depend upon the ability of the club to retain the services of the bulk of the existing squad. The pundits will, undoubtedly, see City as one of the pre-season favourites to make an immediate return, but as Nottingham Forest and Bolton Wanderers have discovered, the route back is never an easy one.

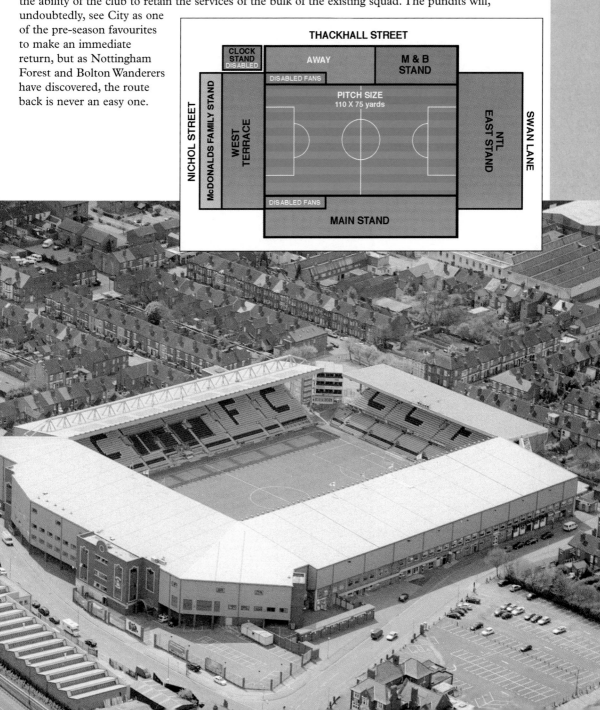

CREWE ALEXANDRA

Gresty Road Ground, Crewe, Cheshire, CW2 6EB

Tel No: 01270 213014
Advance Tickets Tel No: 01270 252610
Fax: 01270 216320
Website: www.crewealex.net
League: 1st Division
Brief History: Founded 1877. Former Grounds: Alexandra Recreation Ground (Nantwich Road), Earle Street Cricket Ground, Edleston Road, Old Sheds Fields, Gresty Road (Adjacent to current Ground), moved to current Ground in 1906. Founder members of 2nd Division (1892) until 1896. Founder members of 3rd Division North (1921). Record attendance 20,000
(Total) Current Capacity: 10,100 all seated
Visiting Supporters' Allocation: 1,736 (BMW Stand)
Club Colours: Red shirts, navy blue shorts
Nearest Railway Station: Crewe

Parking (car): There is a car park adjacent to the ground that is priced at £1.80 for eight hours. It should be noted that there is a residents' only scheme in operation in the streets surrounding the ground.
Parking (Coach/Bus): As directed by Police
Police Force and Tel No: Cheshire (01270 500222)
Disabled Visitors' Facilities:
  Wheelchairs: Available on all four sides
  Blind: Commentary available
Anticipated Development(s): The new main stand was completed for the 1999/2000 season, taking the ground's capacity to 10,000 — and very dramatic it looks too — and this marks the completion of current developments at Gresty Road.

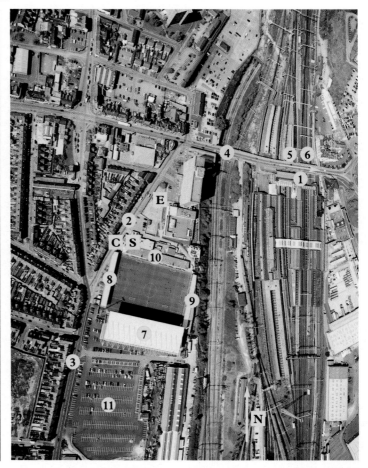

KEY
C Club Offices
S Club Shop
E Entrance(s) for visiting supporters

↑ North direction (approx)

❶ Crewe BR Station
❷ Gresty Road
❸ Gresty Road
❹ A534 Nantwich Road
❺ To A5020 to M6 Junction 16
❻ To M6 Junction 17 [follow directions at roundabout to M6 J16/J17]
❼ Main Stand
❽ Gresty Road (Adtranz) Stand
❾ Railway End
❿ Ringways Stand (BMW)(away)
⓫ Car Park

Above: 684966; Right: 684958

Once again Dario Gradi's Crewe team successfully dragged itself away from the relegation quagmire, although relegation did appear a real threat for much of the season. Despite the team's battle to retain its First Division status, a battle which can often lead to a poor disciplinary record and a 'hoof it and chase it' mentality, Crewe managed to retain its First Division status both with good quality football and a disciplinary record that was second to none. With new talent continuing to emerge from this well-managed team, the club's First Division status should be cemented in 2001/02 by a further display of good quality football.

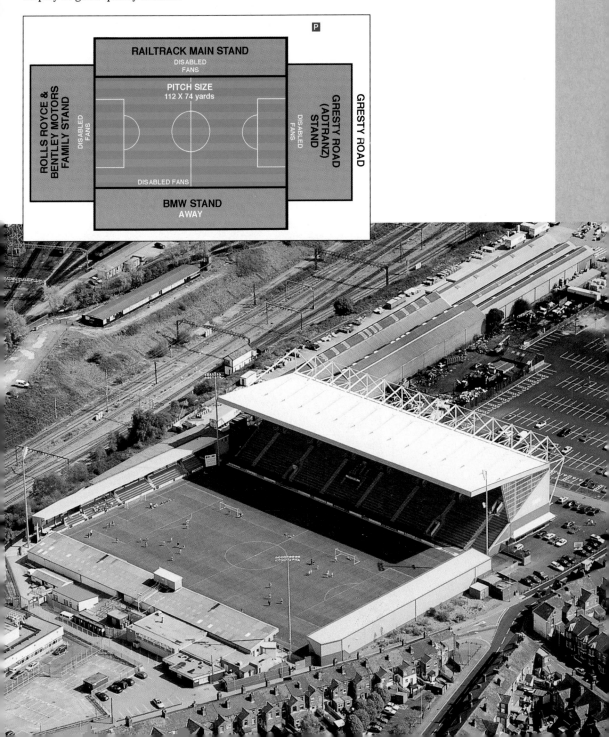

CRYSTAL PALACE

Selhurst Park, London, SE25 6PU

Tel No: 020 8768 6000
Advance Tickets Tel No: 020 8771 8841
Fax: 020 8768 6114
Web Site: www.cpfc.co.uk
E-Mail: palace@cpfc.1.demon.co.uk
Ticket Office/Fax: 020 8653 4708
League: 1st Division
Brief History: Founded 1905. Former Grounds: The Crystal Palace (F.A. Cup Finals venue), London County Athletic Ground (Herne Hill), The Nest (Croydon Common Athletic Ground), moved to Selhurst Park in 1924. Founder members 3rd Division (1920). Record attendance 51,842
(Total) Current Capacity: 26,400 all seated
Visiting Supporters' Allocation: Approx 2,500 in Arthur Wait Stand
Club Colours: Blue and claret striped shirts, red shorts
Nearest Railway Station: Selhurst, Norwood Junction and Thornton Heath

Parking (Car): Street parking and Sainsbury's car park
Parking (Coach/Bus): Thornton Heath
Police Force and Tel No: Metropolitan (020 8653 8568)
Disabled Visitors' Facilities:
Wheelchairs: Arthur Wait and Holmesdale Stands
Blind: Commentary available
Anticipated Development(s): Planning permission has been obtained for the construction of a new Main Stand. As yet there is no confirmed start date. The take-over of the club by Michael Jordan has seen the new owners negotiate a 10-year lease with the Ron Noades-controlled company that owns Selhurst Park. Although too early to say at this stage, this may mean that planned development work will now progress.

KEY

C Club Offices
S Club Shop
E Entrance(s) for visiting supporters
T Toilets for visiting supporters

↑ North direction (approx)

❶ Whitehorse Lane
❷ Park Road
❸ A213 Selhurst Road
❹ Selhurst BR Station (1/2 mile)
❺ Norwood Junction BR Station (1/4 mile)
❻ Thornton Heath BR Station (1/2 mile)
❼ Car Park (Sainsbury's)

Although the arrival of Simon Jordan resulted in the departure of Steve Coppell from the managerial seat it did result in much-needed financial stability at Selhurst Park. From the fans' standpoint, however, it also resulted in the return of Alan Smith to the manager's job resulting in great cup runs but lamentable league form. Palace gradually descended down the league table and were widely considered by the season's end to be almost certain candidates to join QPR and Tranmere in Division Two. In the event, however, the departure of Smith towards the end of April saw a dramatic turnaround in the team's fortunes. An unlikely 4-2 win at fellow strugglers Portsmouth — where defeat would have guaranteed the Eagles' demotion — was followed by a last day win at Stockport County, where Dougie Freedman's 87th minute winner was enough to consign Huddersfield Town to the drop. New manager Steve Bruce will have his work cut out if the Eagles are not to face relegation at the end of 2001/02.

HOLMSDALE ROAD

MAIN STAND

HOLMSDALE ROAD STAND

DISABLED FANS

PITCH SIZE
110 X74 yards

CROYDON ADVERTISER FAMILY STAND

WHITEHORSE LANE

DISABLED FANS

AWAY

ARTHUR WAIT STAND

PARK ROAD

DARLINGTON

Feethams Ground, Darlington, DL1 5JB

Tel No: 01325 240240
Advance Tickets Tel No: 01325 242020
Fax: 01325 240500
Web Site: www.darlingtonfc.net
League: 2nd Division
Brief History: Founded 1883. Founder Members of 3rd Division North (1921), Relegated from 4th Division (1989). Promoted from GM Vauxhall Conference in 1990. Record attendance 21,023
(Total) Current Capacity: 8,379 (3,958 seated)
Visiting Supporters' Allocation: 800 (200 seated)
Club Colours: White and black shirts, black shorts
Nearest Railway Station: Darlington
Parking (Car): Street parking
Parking (Coach/Bus): As directed by Police

Police Force and Tel No: Durham (01325 467681)
Disabled Visitors' Facilities:
　Wheelchairs: 42 spaces available
　Blind: By prior arrangement
Anticipated Development(s): When last year's edition of this book was prepared, the club was confidently expecting work to start on the new stadium at Neasham Road during the course of the season and have it completed by the start of 2001/02. In the event problems over funding the work have led to delays. Currently there would appear to be no definite timetable as to when work will start. Expect the Quakers to have at least one further season at Feethams. The new stadium, which is estimated to cost £7.5 million, will have a 25,000-seat capacity.

KEY

C　Club Offices
S　Club Shop
E　Entrance(s) for visiting supporters
R　Refreshment bars for visiting supporters
T　Toilets for visiting supporters

↑　North direction (approx)

❶　Polam Lane
❷　Victoria Embankment
❸　Feethams Cricket Ground
❹　Victoria Road
❺　Darlington BR Station (¼ mile)
❻　To A1 (M)
❼　East Stand

Above: 680621; *Right:* 680619

One of a number of lower division clubs to have high profile and ambitious owners, Darlington were widely tipped to be amongst those prospering in the Third Division particularly following the club's unlucky defeat in the Play-Off final at the end of the 1999/2000 season. In the event, however, the defeat at Wembley seems to have given the team a season-long hangover and the Quakers struggled for most of it. Never fully being drawn into the relegation mire, 20th place in the Third Division was not what most fans were expecting. The team ought to produce the goods in 2001/02, but there will need to be a dramatic improvement in form if the halcyon days of 1999/2000 are to be recreated.

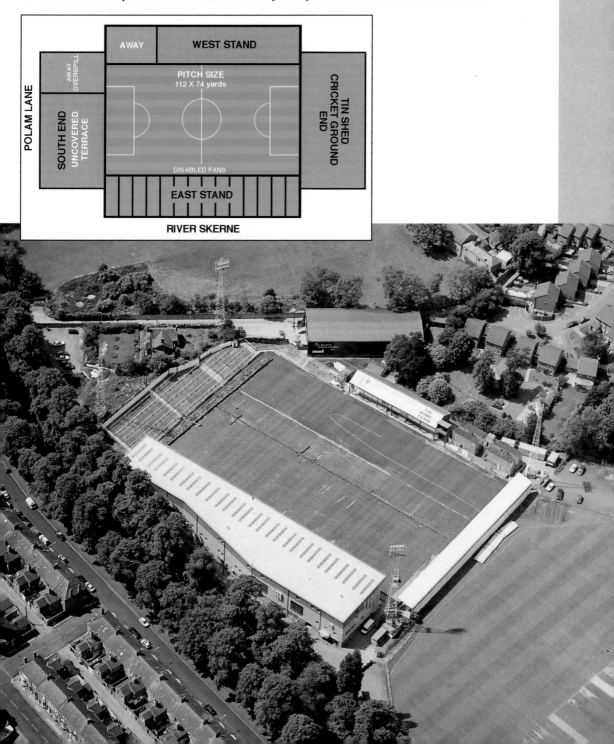

DERBY COUNTY

Pride Park, Derby, Derbyshire DE24 8XL

Tel No: 01332 202202
Advance Tickets Tel No: 01322 209999
Fax: 01322 667540
Web Site: www.dcfc.co.uk
E-Mail: derby.county@dcfc.co.uk
League: F.A. Premiership
Brief History: Founded 1884. Former grounds: The Racecourse Ground, the Baseball Ground (1894-1997), moved to Pride Park 1997. Founder members of the Football League (1888). Record capacity at the Baseball Ground: 41,826; at Pride Park: 32,916
(Total) Current Capacity: 33,258
Visiting Supporters' Allocation: 4,800 in the South Stand
Club Colours: White shirts and black shorts

Nearest Railway Station: Derby
Parking (Car): 2,300 places at the ground designated for season ticket holders. Also two 1,000 car parks on the A6/A52 link road. No on-street parking
Parking (Coach/Bus): As directed
Police Force and Tel No: Derbyshire (01332 290100)
Disabled Visitors' Facilities:
  Wheelchairs: 70 home/30 away spaces
  Blind: Commentary available
Anticipated Development(s): There are no definite plans for the further development of Pride Park following the completion of the southwest corner.

KEY

C Club Offices
S Club Shop
E Entrance(s) for visiting supporters

⬆ North direction (approx)

❶ To Derby Midland BR station
❷ North Stand
❸ West Stand
❹ South (Mansfield Bitter) Stand (away)
❺ East Stand
❻ Derwent Parade
❼ To A52/M1
❽ To City Centre and A6
❾ A52

Above: 679691; *Right:* 679687

At the start of the season many pundits regarded Jim Smith's team as one of the prime candidates for relegation and early season form tended to confirm the view that time was running out for County in the Premiership. However, the appointment of Colin West as Smith's Number Two and the arrival of flesh blood in the squad, with players like Taribo West appearing, caused a considerable revival in the latter part of the season. Mathematically, however, the club's Premiership survival was only ensured for another season following the unlikely defeat of Manchester United at Old Trafford — only the second home game that United had lost all season — in early May. Thus the Bald Eagle's team lives to battle it out in the Premiership for another season; fans should, however, anticipate a further battle to avoid the drop in 2001/02.

PIRELII STAND

WEST TOYOTA STAND

PITCH SIZE
115 x 75 yards

MANSFIELD BITTER STAND

AWAY

McDONALD'S COMMUNITY NORTH (SINGING) STAND

DISABLED

EAST STAND

DISABLED

P

EVERTON

Goodison Park, Goodison Road, Liverpool, L4 4EL

Tel No: 0151 330 2200
Advance Tickets Tel No: 0151 330 2300
Fax: 0151 286 9112
Web Site: www.evertonfc.com
E-Mail: webmaster@evertonfc.com
League: F.A. Premier
Brief History: Founded 1879 as St. Domingo, changed to Everton in 1880. Former grounds: Stanley Park, Priory Road and Anfield (Liverpool F.C. Ground), moved to Goodison Park in 1892. Founder-members Football League (1888). Record attendance 78,299
(Total) Current Capacity: 40,260 all seated
Visiting Supporters' Allocation: 2,726
Club Colours: Blue and white shirts, white shorts
Nearest Railway Station: Liverpool Lime Street
Parking (Car): Corner of Utting and Priory Avenues

Parking (Coach/Bus): Priory Road
Police Force and Tel No: Merseyside (0151 709 6010)
Disabled Visitors' Facilities:
Wheelchairs: Bullens Road Stand
Blind: Commentary available
Anticipated Development(s): The on-off saga of the club's possible relocation is now definitely back on. A poll of fans in early 2001 indicated a high level of support for the project and the club is investigating the possibilities of constructing a new 55,000-seat capacity ground in the King's Dock area of the city. The relocation project will see the club move by the start of the 2003/04 season with the new ground costing an estimated £155 million.

KEY

- **C** Club Offices
- **S** Club Shop
- **E** Entrance(s) for visiting supporters
- **R** Refreshment bars for visiting supporters
- **T** Toilets for visiting supporters

↑ North direction (approx)

❶ A580 Walton Road
❷ Bullen Road
❸ Goodison Road
❹ Car Park
❺ Liverpool Lime Street BR Station (2 miles)
❻ To M57 Junction 2, 4 and 5
❼ Stanley Park

Historically considered to be amongst the traditional 'Big Five' of English football, it is a long time since Everton were in a position to challenge seriously for any major trophy and, once again, in 2000/01 the club was more concerned with affairs at the wrong end of the Premiership table. With several of Walter Smith's experienced veterans departing during the close season — Richard Gough into retirement and Dave Watson to take over the Tranmere hot seat — the club will face 2001/02 with a certain degree of concern. There are undoubtedly talented players in the squad; the concerns must be for fans that there may not be enough to ensure Premiership survival one further time.

EXETER CITY

St. James Park, Exeter, EX4 6PX

Tel No: 01392 254073
Advance Tickets Tel No: 01392 254073
Fax: 01392 425885
Web Site: www.exetercityfc.co.uk
League: 3rd Division
Brief History: Founded in 1904. (From amalgamation of St. Sidwell United and Exeter United.) Founder-members Third Division (1920). Record attendance 20,984
(Total) Current Capacity: 9,036 (3,865 seated)
Visiting Supporters' Allocation: 1,200 (in St James' Road Terrace) (0 seated)
Club Colours: Red and white striped shirts, white shorts
Nearest Railway Station: Exeter St. James Park
Parking (Car): National Car Park and Council Car Parks (No street parking)
Parking (Coach/Bus): Paris Street bus station

Police Force and Tel No: Devon and Cornwall (01392 52101)
Disabled Visitors' Facilities:
  Wheelchairs: St James Road entrance (prior booking
  Blind: No special facility
Anticipated Development(s): With the completion of the Cliff Bastin Stand (capacity 3,971 standing; opened February 2000) and of the Doble Stand (2,175 seated on the site of the former Cowshed), the club has long term plans to redevelop the remaining two sides of the ground, although there is no definite time scale at the present time. The next phase of redevelopment will see the site of the former St James' school rebuilt into The St James' Centre, which will house the social club and conference facilities.

KEY

E Entrance(s) for visiting supporters

R Refreshment bars for visiting supporters

T Toilets for visiting supporters

⬆ North direction (approx)

❶ Exeter St. James Park BR Station
❷ St. James Road
❸ Old Tiverton Road
❹ Blackboy Road
❺ Well Street
❻ St James Road End (away)
❼ Big Bank Stand
❽ Cowshed Stand

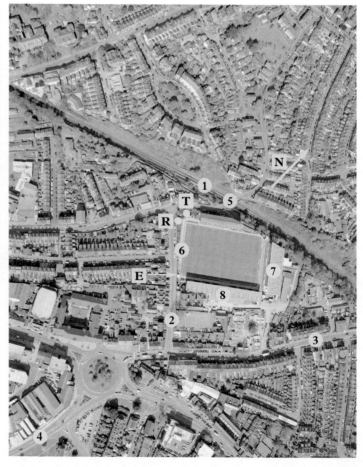

Above: 688406; *Right:* 688403

For much of the season it looked as though the redeveloped facilities at the other St James' Park would grace the Nationwide Conference rather than the Third Division as Noel Blake's team hovered at or near the bottom of the division. However, the team managed to drag itself away from the bottom of the table and finished slightly higher than in 1999-2000. Unless fortunes improve dramatically, however, fans can expect another torrid season with potentially a struggle against local rivals Torquay United to avoid the drop to the Conference.

OLD TIVERTON ROAD

DOBLE STAND

CLIFF BASTIN STAND
COVERED TERRACE

PITCH SIZE
113 X 71 yards

DISABLED
FANS

St JAMES ROAD END
UNCOVERED TERRACE
AWAY

St JAMES ROAD

MAIN GRANDSTAND

FULHAM

Craven Cottage, Stevenage Road, Fulham, London, SW6 6HH

Tel No: 020 7893 8383
Advance Tickets Tel No: 020 7384 4710
Fax: 020 7384 4715
Web Site: www.fulhamfc.co.uk
League: FA Premier
Brief History: Founded in 1879 as St. Andrews Fulham, changed name to Fulham in 1898. Former Grounds: Star Road, Ranelagh Club, Lillie Road, Eel Brook Common, Purser's Cross, Barn Elms and Half Moon (Wasps Rugby Football Ground), moved to Craven Cottage in 1894. Record attendance 49,335
(Total) Current Capacity: 18,623 (7,023 seated)
Visiting Supporters' Allocation: 4,600 (600 seated) in Riverside Stand and Putney Terrace
Club Colours: White shirts, black shorts
Nearest Railway Station: Putney Bridge (Tube)
Parking (Car): Street parking
Parking (Coach/Bus): Stevenage Road
Police Force and Tel No: Metropolitan (020 7741 6212)

Disabled Visitors' Facilities:
Wheelchairs: Main Stand and Hammersmith End
Blind: No special facility
Anticipated Development(s): With Fulham's promotion to the Premiership, terraces will make a return to top flight football for Craven Cottage's final season before redevelopment. The club has ambitious plans for the reconstruction of the ground with planning permission being granted towards the end of the 2000-01 season for the construction of a 30,000 all-seater stadium costing £55 million on the existing site. All of the existing ground — including the famous cottage — will be swept away with the exception of the facade along Stevenage Road. It is anticipated that work will commence at the end of the 2001/02 season with Fulham ground sharing during the 2002/03 season, prior to occupying its new facility in August 2003.

KEY

E Entrance(s) for visiting supporters

R Refreshment bars for visiting supporters

T Toilets for visiting supporters

↑ North direction (approx)

❶ River Thames
❷ Stevenage Road
❸ Finlay Street
❹ Putney Bridge Tube Station (½ mile)
❺ Putney Terrace
❻ Riverside Stand
❼ Main Stand
❽ Hammersmith End
❾ Craven Cottage

68 *Above:* 685839; *Right:* 685834

A combination of Mohammed Al-Fayed's money and Jean Tigana's managerial skill was always likely to bring renewed success to Craven Cottage and, in the event, fans were not disappointed. Good runs in both the Worthington and FA cups were, however, merely the icing on the cake for a hugely successful league campaign that saw Fulham run away with the First Division championship with over 100 points. Equally impressive was the club's formidable striking partnerships, with Saha grabbing more than 30 goals during the season and the club averaging about two goals per game in the league. Pride in the team's success, bringing top flight football to the cottage for the first time in more than 30 years, will, however, be tempered by the reality that other promoted teams have struggled and that many of the squad have yet to prove themselves in top-class football. Much of Fulham's future will depend on how far Al-Fayed is prepared to dig into his pocket to guarantee Premiership survival.

GILLINGHAM

Priestfield Stadium, Redfern Avenue, Gillingham, Kent, ME7 4DD

Tel No: 01634 300000
Advance Tickets Tel No: 01634 851854
Fax: 01634 850986
Web Site: gillinghamfootballclub.com
E-mail: information@gillinghamfootballclub.com
League: 1st Division
Brief History: Founded 1893, as New Brompton, changed name to Gillingham in 1913. Founder-members Third Division (1920). Lost Football League status (1938), re-elected to Third Division South (1950). Record attendance 23,002
(Total) Current Capacity: 14,325 (10,525 seated)
Visiting Supporters' Allocation: 1,800 (in Redfern Terrace Avenue Corner Terrace)
Club Colours: Blue and Black striped shirts, black shorts

Nearest Railway Station: Gillingham
Parking (Car): Street parking
Parking (Coach/Bus): As directed by Police
Police Force and Tel No: Kent (01634 834488)
Disabled Visitors' Facilities:
   Wheelchairs: Redfern Avenue
   Blind: No special facility
Anticipated Development(s): Following completion of the new Medway (Main) Stand, the only part of the Priestfield Stadium that awaits attention is the open Gillingham End. However, the club has long term plans to relocate —a site in Strood is one possibility — and so don't expect any dramatic changes until a final decision is made. The club has until the start of the 2003/04 season to become all-seater, assuming that it retains its First Division status.

KEY

E Entrance(s) for visiting supporters

↑ North direction (approx)

❶ Redfern Avenue
❷ Toronto Road
❸ Gordon Road
❹ Gillingham BR station (¼ mile)
❺ Gordon Street Stand
❻ New two-tier Main (Medway) Stand
❼ New Rainham End Stand
❽ Gillingham End; uncovered terrace

Above: 688418; *Right:* 688412

Now under player-manager Andy Hessenthaler, the Gills' first season in the First Division was one of considerable progress as the team established itself well at the higher level despite being heavily tipped for an immediate return to the Second Division. Finishing in mid-table can be considered a success, considering how many promoted teams struggle to retain their newly won status. However, it is likely that Gillingham will face a stronger challenge to the team's First Division position in 2001/02.

GRIMSBY TOWN

Blundell Park, Cleethorpes, DN35 7PY

Tel No: 01472 605050
Advance Tickets Tel No: 01472 605050
Fax: 01472 693665
Web Site: www.gtfc.co.uk
E-Mail: mariners@gcfc.co.uk
League: 1st Division
Brief History: Founded in 1878, as Grimsby Pelham, changed name to Grimsby Town in 1879. Former Grounds: Clee Park (two adjacent fields) and Abbey Park, moved to Blundell Park in 1899. Founder-members 2nd Division (1892). Record attendance 31,651
(Total) Current Capacity: 10,033 (all seated)
Visiting Supporters' Allocation: 1,874
Club Colours: Black and white striped shirts, black shorts

Nearest Railway Station: Cleethorpes
Parking (Car): Street parking
Parking (Coach/Bus): Harrington Street
Police Force and Tel No: Humberside (01472 359171)
Disabled Visitors' Facilities:
  Wheelchairs: Harrington Street
  Blind: Commentary available
Anticipated Development(s): Time is running out for Blundell Park as the club has ambitious plans for the construction of a new 20,000-seat ground at Great Coates. If all goes according to plan, work is scheduled to start in September 2001 with the new ground being available for the start of the 2002/03 season.

KEY

C Club Offices
S Club Shop
E Entrance(s) for visiting supporters
R Refreshment bars for visiting supporters
T Toilets for visiting supporters

↑ North direction (approx)

❶ A180 Grimsby Road
❷ Cleethorpes BR Station (1½ miles)
❸ To Grimsby and M180 Junction 5
❹ Harrington Street
❺ Constitutional Avenue
❻ Humber Estuary

A disappointing season for the Mariners again saw the team flirting with relegation from the Second Division. Indeed, if results had gone against the team on the final Sunday, then Grimsby could well have been joining QPR and Huddersfield Town in the Second Division. In the event, however, victory at home over champions Fulham meant that Lennie Lawrence's side finished in 18th position, a slight improvement over that achieved in 1999/2000. However, fans can no doubt expect another season of struggle if Second Division football is not to greet the new stadium.

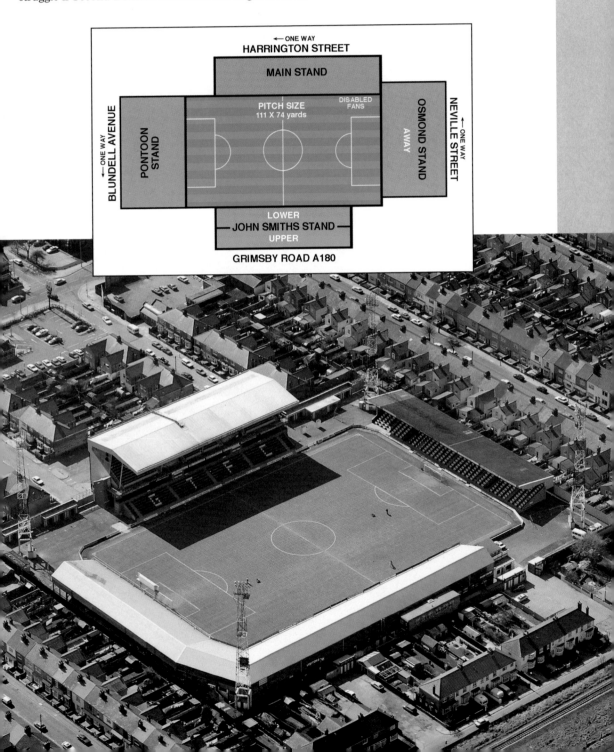

HALIFAX TOWN

Shay Ground, Halifax, West Yorkshire HX1 2YS

Tel No: 01422 341222
Advance Tickets Tel No: 01422 341222
Fax: 01422 349487
Web Site: www.halifaxafc.co.uk
E-mail: theshay@halifaxafc.co.uk
League: 3rd Division
Brief History: Founded 1911; elected to the Football League in 1921. Relegated from the Football League to Vauxhall Conference at the end of the 1992/93 season; won Vauxhall Conference title and promoted to Third Division in 1997/98. Record attendance 36,885
(Total) Current Capacity: 9,927 (1,830 seated)
Visiting Supporters' Allocation: 3,800 in North Stand
Club Colours: Blue and white shirts, blue and white shorts
Nearest Railway Station: Halifax
Parking (Car): There is a car park at the ground; access for pass holders only. Also car park at the corner of Skircoat Road and Hunger Hill. Also street parking
Parking (Coach/Bus): As directed
Police Force and Tel No: West Yorkshire (01422 3603333)
Disabled Visitors' Facilities:
   Wheelchairs: Approximately 36 places
   Blind: Commentary available
Anticipated Development(s): Following completion of the new Main Stand, taking the ground's capacity to 12,000, three sides of The Shay will have been rebuilt since the club's promotion back to the League in 1998. Future work will involve the reconstruction of the Skircoat Road Stand, which will result ultimately in the ground possessing a 15,000 capacity. The work is being undertaken in conjunction with the ground's owners (Calderdale MBC) and with the co-tenants, Halifax Blue Sox RLFC.

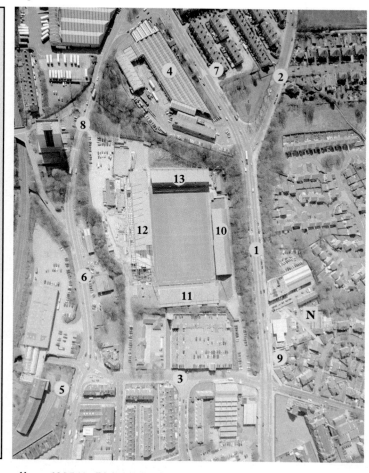

KEY

↑ North direction (approx)

❶ Skircoat Road
❷ Heath Road
❸ Hunger Hill
❹ Bus Depot
❺ To station (0.5 miles)
❻ Shaw Syke
❼ To M62 (Junction 24) via A629
❽ Shaw Hill
❾ To Town Centre (0.25 miles)
❿ Skircoat Stand
⓫ North Stand
⓬ Main Stand (under construction)
⓭ South Stand

Above: 688569; *Right:* 688563

As widely expected, last season was again a battle against relegation back to the Conference for Town, a club now managed by ex-Fulham boss Paul Bracewell. With four or five teams — Exeter, Lincoln, Carlisle, Torquay and Barnet — along with Halifax all involved in the relegation dog-fight, it came as a considerable relief that Halifax's survival did not depend on any decent result from the last match of the season — away at high-flying Chesterfield. In the event, a 3-0 defeat meant that the Shaymen were to finish penultimate in the Third Division and, unless fortunes improve dramatically, the Calderdale faithful can expect another stressful season in 2001/02.

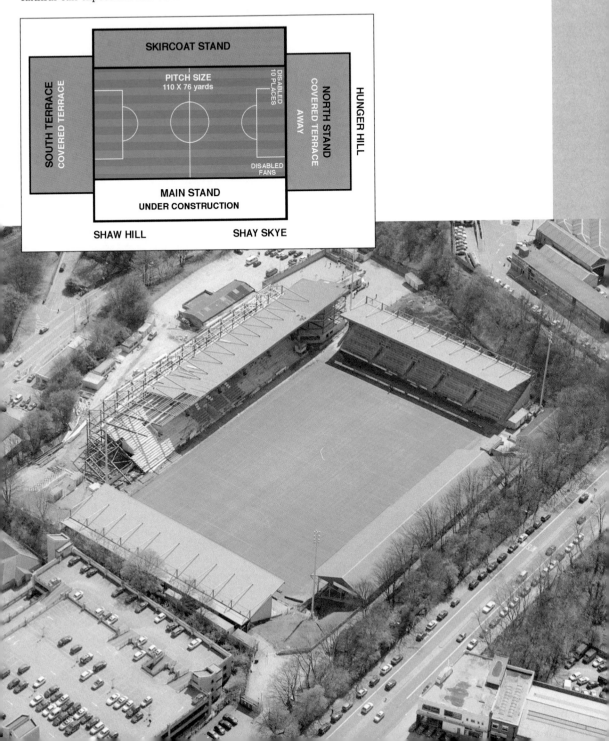

SKIRCOAT STAND

PITCH SIZE
110 X 76 yards

SOUTH TERRACE
COVERED TERRACE

DISABLED
10 PLACES

NORTH STAND
COVERED TERRACE
AWAY

HUNGER HILL

DISABLED
FANS

MAIN STAND
UNDER CONSTRUCTION

SHAW HILL   SHAY SKYE

HARTLEPOOL UNITED

Victoria Park, Clarence Road, Hartlepool, TS24 8BZ

Tel No: 01429 272584
Advance Tickets Tel No: 01429 272584
Web Site: www.hartlepoolunited.co.uk
E-Mail: info@hartlepoolunited.co.uk
Fax: 01429 863007
League: 3rd Division
Brief History: Founded 1808 as Hartlepools United, changed to Hartlepool (1968) and to Hartlepool United in 1977. Founder-members 3rd Division (1921). Record attendance 17,426
(Total) Current Capacity: 7,229 (3,966 seated)
Visiting Supporters' Allocation: 741 (located in Rink Stand)
Club Colours: Blue and white striped shirts, blue shorts

Nearest Railway Station: Hartlepool Church Street
Parking (Car): Street parking and rear of clock garage
Parking (Coach/Bus): As directed
Police Force and Tel No: Cleveland (01429 221151
Disabled Visitors' Facilities:
  Wheelchairs: Cyril Knowles Stand
  Blind: Commentary available
Anticipated Development(s): The plans for the redevelopment of the Millhouse Stand are still progressing, although there is now no definite timescale. When this work does commence, the ground's capacity will be reduced to 5,000.

KEY

C Club Offices
S Club Shop
E Entrance(s) for visiting supporters

↑ North direction (approx)

❶ A179 Clarence Road
❷ Hartlepool Church Street BR Station
❸ Marina Way
❹ Site of former Greyhound Stadium
❺ To Middlesbrough A689 & A1(M)
❻ To A19 North
❼ Rink Stand

Above: 680637; *Right:* 680641

A season of some success for United saw Chris Turner's team again reach the Play-Offs (for the second successive season), finishing fourth. However, once again the Play-Offs proved a competition too far for the team, as defeat by seventh placed Blackpool over the two legs of the Semi-Final once again consigned United to Third Division football. However, there is the potential for the team to build on the success of the previous two seasons and mount a meaningful campaign in 2001/02 for either automatic promotion or the Play-Offs.

HUDDERSFIELD TOWN

The Alfred McAlpine Stadium, Leeds Road, Huddersfield, HD1 6PX

Tel No: 01484 484100
Advance Tickets Tel No: 01484 484123
Fax: 01484 484101
Web Site: www.htafc.com
E-Mail: ht.afc@virgin.net
League: 2nd Division
Brief History: Founded 1908, elected to Football League in 1910. First Club to win the Football League Championship three years in succession. Moved from Leeds Road ground to Kirklees (Alfred McAlpine) Stadium 1994/95 season. Record attendance (Leeds Road) 67,037; McAlpine Stadium: 22,129
(Total) Current Capacity: 24,000 (all seated)
Visiting Supporters' Allocation: 4,037 (all seated)

Club Colours: Blue and white striped shirts , white shorts
Nearest Railway Station: Huddersfield
Parking (Car): Car parks adjacent to ground
Parking (Coach/Bus): Car parks adjacent to ground
Police Force and Tel No: West Yorkshire (01484 422122)
Disabled Visitors' Facilities:
  Wheelchairs: Three sides of Ground, at low levels and raised area, including toilet access
  Blind: Area for Partially sighted with Hospital Radio commentary
Anticipated Development(s): With completion of the new North Stand, work on the McAlpine Stadium is over.

KEY

C Club Offices
S Club Shop
E Entrance(s) for visiting supporters

⬆ North direction (approx)

❶ To Leeds and M62 Junction 25
❷ A62 Leeds Road
❸ To Huddersfield BR station (1¼ miles)
❹ Disabled parking
❺ Town Avenue pay car park (on site of former ground)
❻ North Stand
❼ St Andrews pay car park
❽ Coach park
❾ South Stand (away)

Above: 679683; *Right:* 679681

At the start of the season, the Terriers were widely considered to be candidates for the Play-Off spots, even if automatic promotion was considered unlikely, given the fact that at the end of the 1999/2000 season the team had only just missed out on the Play-Offs. In the event, however, Steve Bruce's team failed to live up to expectations and the manager was ultimately to pay for this failure. His replacement, Lou Macari (who inherited the team when it was rooted to the bottom), caused a mini-revival but it all went disastrously wrong for the team on the final day of the season when wins for both Crystal Palace and Portsmouth, allied to a 2-1 home defeat by Birmingham City, consigned Town to the Second Division. The Terriers have the potential to make an immediate return and fans will certainly be expecting them to have but a single season in the Second Division.

HULL CITY

Boothferry Park, Boothferry Road, Hull, HU4 6EU

Tel No: 01482 575263
Advance Tickets Tel No: 01482 506660
Fax: 01482 565752
Web Site: www.hullcityafc.net
E-Mail: info@hullcity.org.uk
League: 3rd Division
Brief History: Founded 1904. Former grounds:
The Boulevard (Hull Rugby League Ground),
Dairycoates, Anlaby Road Cricket Circle (Hull
Cricket Ground), Anlaby Road, moved to
Boothferry Park in 1946. Record attendance
55,019
(Total) Current Capacity: 15,160 (5,262
seated)
Visiting Supporters' Allocation: 1,859 (535
seated)
Club Colours: Amber with black and white
trim shirts, black shorts

Nearest Railway Station: Hull Paragon
Parking (Car): Street Parking and at ground
(limited)
Parking (Coach/Bus): At ground
Police Force and Tel No: Humberside (01482
220148)
Disabled Visitors' Facilities:
Wheelchairs: Corner East/South stands
Blind: Commentary available
Anticipated Development(s): It looks as
though relocation is on the cards for Hull City
with the local council proposing a new £43.5
million stadium to be shared between football
and Rugby League. The new stadium would be
built at the Circle, an area of parkland to the
west of the city. There is, however, no
confirmed schedule for this work.

KEY

C Club Offices
S Club Shop
E Entrance(s) for visiting
supporters

↑ North direction (approx)

❶ A63 Boothferry Road
❷ North Road
❸ Hull Paragon BR Station
(1 1/2 miles)
❹ To Humber Bridge and M62
Junction 38

Above: 612976; *Right:* 612986

A season of some success on the field matched with tribulation off it, saw the Tigers reach the Play-Offs despite all sorts of problems financially. At one stage during the season it looked a very real possibility that the team would fold as the ground was locked against it and financial problems mounted. With Boothferry Park locked, there was even a possibility that home games might have been played across the Humber at Grimsby. In the event, the crisis was averted as new owners took over. On the field, whilst a Play-Off spot was achieved, defeat by Leyton Orient saw the Tigers consigned to another season of Third Division fare. However, given the traumas of 2000/01, the fact that football is being played in the city will be satisfaction enough for most fans and, if the same sort of progress can be made on the field during 2001/02, then there ought to much optimism in Hull for the coming campaign.

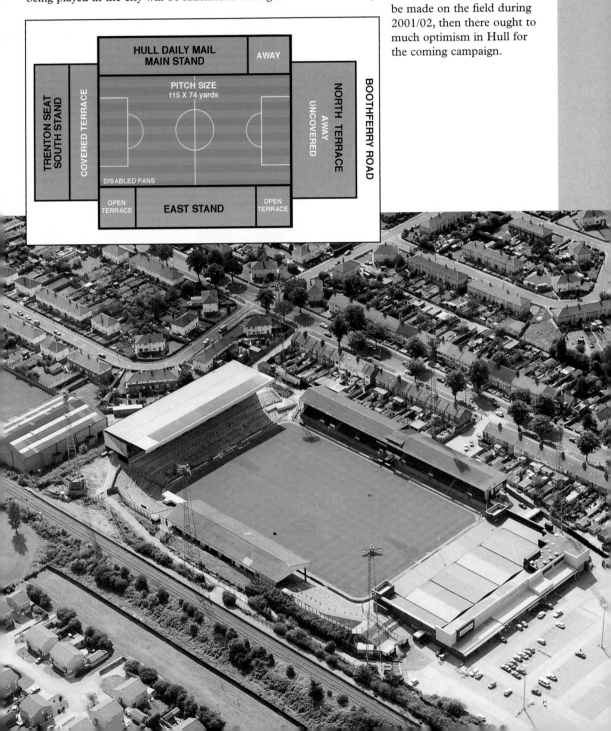

IPSWICH TOWN

Portman Road, Ipswich, IP1 2DA

Tel No: 01473 400500
Advance Tickets Tel No: 0845 6050129
Fax: 01473 400040
Web Site: http://www.itfc.co.uk
E-Mail: enquiries@itfc.co.uk
League: FA Premier League
Brief History: Founded 1887 as Ipswich Association F.C., changed to Ipswich Town in 1888. Former Grounds: Broom Hill & Brookes Hall, moved to Portman Road in 1888. Record attendance 38,010
(Total) Current Capacity: 22,600 all seated
Visiting Supporters' Allocation: 1,771 all seated in Cobbold Stand
Club Colours: Blue shirts, white shorts
Nearest Railway Station: Ipswich

Parking (Car): Portman Road, Portman Walk & West End Road
Parking (Coach/Bus): West End Road
Police Force and Tel No: Suffolk (01473 611611)
Disabled Visitors' Facilities:
  Wheelchairs: Lower Pioneer Stand
  Blind: Commentary available
Anticipated Development(s): Work started on the reconstruction of the South (Churchman's) Stand during the course of the 2000/01 season. Conditional planning permission has been granted for the construction of a new North Stand. When completed, this will take Portman Road's capacity to 30,000.

KEY

C Club Offices
S Club Shop
E Entrance(s) for visiting supporters
R Refreshment bars for visiting supporters
T Toilets for visiting supporters

↑ North direction (approx)

❶ A137 West End Road
❷ Portman Walk
❸ Portman Road
❹ Princes Street
❺ To Ipswich BR Station
❻ Car Parks
❼ Cobbold Stand
❽ West Stand
❾ North Stand
❿ Churchmans (South) Stand

Above: 687743; *Right:* 687734

Widely tipped as automatic candidates for relegation — a prophesy that looked all too likely when the team crashed 4-1 away at Tottenham in the first game of the season — George Burley's side proved to be one of the surprise packets of the season. With strikers such as Marcus Stewart proving that they could score freely at the highest level, the team was to achieve a place guaranteeing a spot in the 2001/02 UEFA Cup and only just failed to make the Champions League. Finishing in such a position is without doubt a considerable success; the danger must be that, with more games likely next season as the team progresses through various cup competitions, injuries will mount up. Next season's Premiership is likely to be much tougher than that in 2000/01 — with both Liverpool and Leeds becoming powerhouses again — and fans will be hoping that the Tractor Boys can ensure that this season's success was not a one-year wonder.

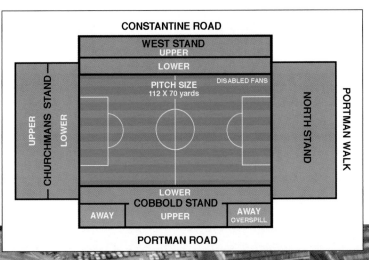

KIDDERMINSTER HARRIERS

Aggborough Stadium, Hoo Road, Kidderminster, Worcestershire DY10 1NB

Tel No: 01562 823931
Advance Tickets Tel No: 01562 823931
Fax: 01562 827329
Web Site: http://www.harriers.co.uk
E-Mail: info@harriers.co.uk
League: 3rd Division
Brief History: The club was established in
1886. There have been no previous grounds.
The team won the Nationwide Conference
title at the end of the 1999/2000 season and
entered the Nationwide League for 2000/01
season. Record attendance at Aggborough
Stadium: 9,155
(Total) Current Capacity: 6,237 (1,107
seated)
Visiting Supporters' Allocation: 1,300 (all
unseated in South [College End] Terrace)
Club Colours: Red shirts with white markings;
red shorts

Nearest Railway Station: Kidderminster
Parking (Car): Limited at ground parking
otherwise on-street
Parking (Coach/Bus): As directed
Police Force and Tel No: West Mercia (01562
820888
Disabled Visitors' Facilities:
Wheelchairs: Designated section in front of
George Reynolds Stand
Blind: No special facility
Anticipated Development(s): There are plans
to construct a new 2,500-seat stand — again to
be named after Bill Grieves — opposite the
existing Main Stand. However, whether this
development progresses will be determined by
the size of the crowds the club attracts.

KEY

C Club Offices
S Club Shop
E Entrance(s) for visiting
   supporters

↑ North direction (approx)

❶ South (College) End – away
❷ Kidderminster Town station
   (Severn Valley Railway)
❸ Kidderminster station
❹ Hoo Road
❺ Constitution Hill Ringway
❻ To Town Centre (half a mile)
❼ Chester Road South
❽ To A449 and M5 (14 miles)
❾ Stadium Close
❿ Car park
⓫ Harriers Trading Estate
⓬ Vicarage Close

Above: 685564; *Right:* 685558

Harriers' first season in the Nationwide League brought a mid-table position for Jan Molby's team. Unlike other teams promoted from the Conference — most notably Macclesfield and Cheltenham — the team never threatened seriously to get involved in the battle for promotion. However, with the club now consolidated in the Football League, the good burghers of Kidderminster can look forward to more local derbies against Shrewsbury Town and the possibility of more football specials on the adjacent Severn Valley Railway.

HOO ROAD

GEORGE REYNOLDS
STAND

PITCH SIZE
112 X 72 yards

DISABLED

SOUTH
(COLLEGE END)
TERRACE
(COVERED)
AWAY

TOWN END
TERRACE
(COVERED)

WILLIAM GREAVES STAND
(COW SHED)

LEEDS UNITED

Elland Road, Leeds, LS11 0ES

Tel No: 0113 226 6000
Advance Tickets Tel No: 0113 226 1000
Fax: 0113 226 6050
Web Site: www.lufc.co.uk
E-mail: admin@lufc.co.uk
League: F.A. Premier
Brief History: Founded 1919, formed from the former 'Leeds City' Club, who were disbanded following expulsion from the Football League in October 1919. Joined Football League in 1920. Record attendance 57,892
(Total) Current Capacity: 40,294 (all seated)
Visiting Supporters' Allocation: 1,725 in South East Corner (can be increased to 3,662 in South Stand if necessary)
Club Colours: White shirts, white shorts

Nearest Railway Station: Leeds City
Parking (Car): Car parks adjacent to ground
Parking (Coach/Bus): As directed by Police
Police Force and Tel No: West Yorkshire (0113 243 5353)
Disabled Visitors' Facilities:
  Wheelchairs: West Stand and South Stand
  Blind: Commentary available
Anticipated Development(s): The club announced at the end of the season that it was investigating either the further redevelopment of Elland Road in order to expand capacity or to relocate. There are, however, no detailed plans at the moment and expect the situation to stay unchanged for at least 2001/02.

KEY
C Club Offices
S Club Shop
E Entrance(s) for visiting supporters

⬆ North direction (approx)

❶ M621
❷ M621 Junction 2
❸ A643 Elland Road
❹ Lowfields Road
❺ To A58
❻ City Centre and BR station
❼ To M62 and M1

A curate's egg of a season for David O'Leary's talented squad saw the team thrive in the Champions League, reaching further in the competition than either the much fancied Arsenal or Manchester United, but fail to start a serious challenge in the league until almost the New Year. Although the team managed to get itself into a position to challenge for a further Champions League spot, this was, however, not be to be achieved and European competition at Elland Road in 2001/02 will be in the form of the UEFA Cup. With a strong squad of players and, apparently, a sizeable cheque book for strengthening it — witness the £18 million spent on Rio Ferdinand — United look capable of mounting a challenge for the championship this season — provided that they remember that the competition begins with the first game of the season and not at Christmas.

LEICESTER CITY

City Stadium, Filbert Street, Leicester, LE2 7FL

Tel No: 0116 291 5000/5098
Advance Tickets Tel No: 0116 291 5296
Fax: 0116 247 0585
Web Site: www.lcfc.co.uk
E-mail: abby.worsnip@lcfc.co.uk
League: F.A. Premier
Brief History: Founded 1884 as Leicester Fosse, changed name to Leicester City in 1919. Former Grounds: Fosse Road South, Victoria Road, Belgrave Cycle Track, Mill Lane and Aylestone Road Cricket Ground, moved to Filbert Street in 1891. Record attendance 47,298
(Total) Current Capacity: 21,500 (all seated)
Visiting Supporters' Allocation: 2,011 in East Stand Blocks T and U

Club Colours: Blue shirts, white shorts
Nearest Railway Station: Leicester
Parking (Car): NCP car park and street parking
Parking (Coach/Bus): Western Boulevard
Police Force and Tel No: Leicester (0116 253 0066)
Disabled Visitors' Facilities:
  Wheelchairs: 67 places in Carling, South and East Stands
  Blind: Commentary available
Anticipated Development(s): The proposals for the construction of a new stadium at Freemans Wharf have been resurrected although the actual time-scale is still to be confirmed.

KEY

C Club Offices
S Club Shop
E Entrance(s) for visiting supporters
R Refreshment bars for visiting supporters
T Toilets for visiting supporters

↑ North direction (approx)

❶ Walnut Street
❷ Filbert Street
❸ Grasmere Street
❹ River Soar
❺ M1 and M69 Junction 21
❻ Leicester BR Station (1 mile)

For the first few months of the season it seemed that the Foxes and Peter Taylor were a winning combination, as the team stormed to the higher echelons of the Premiership. However, come the New Year, the team's form slipped dramatically, typified by a home defeat against Second Division Wycombe Wanderers in the FA Cup. Towards the end of the season, an eight-game losing run could almost have resulted in City being sucked into the relegation battle if enough points had not been gathered earlier. A 4-2 victory at Filbert Street in the penultimae game of the season brought the series of defeats to an end but 2000/01 will be looked back on by the fans as one of missed opportunities. With Southampton having relocated, only Fulham will have a smaller capacity in 2001/02 and all the evidence suggests that ultimately it will be the clubs with the smaller capacities that will struggle. Fans of the Foxes may have to prepare themselves for a renewed acquaintance with the relegation dog-fight.

LEYTON ORIENT

Matchroom Stadium, Brisbane Road, Leyton, London, E10 5NE

Tel No: 020 8926 1111
Advance Tickets Tel No: 020 8926 1010
Fax: 020 8926 1110
Web Site: http://leytonorient.com
E-Mail: orient@bigfoot.com
League: 3rd Division
Brief History: Founded 1887 as Clapton Orient, from Eagle Cricket Club (formerly Glyn Cricket Club formed in 1881). Changed name to Leyton Orient (1946), Orient (1966), Leyton Orient (1987). Former grounds: Glyn Road, Whittles Athletic Ground, Millfields Road, Lea Bridge Road, Wembley Stadium (2 games), moved to Brisbane Road in 1937. Record attendance 34,345
(Total) Current Capacity: 13,677 (9,387 seated)

Visiting Supporters' Allocation: 2,154 (932 seated) in East Stand/Terrace
Club Colours: Red shirts, red shorts
Nearest Railway Station: Leyton (tube), Leyton Midland Road
Parking (Car): Street parking
Parking (Coach/Bus): As directed by Police
Police Force and Tel No: Metropolitan (020 8556 8855)
Disabled Visitors' Facilities:
  Wheelchairs: Windsor Road
  Blind: Match commentary supplied on request
Anticipated Development(s): The next stage in the redevelopment at Brisbane Road is for the construction of a new West Stand, for which the team was granted £1 million by the Football Trust in December 2000.

KEY
C Club Offices
S Club Shop
E Entrance(s) for visiting supporters

↑ North direction (approx)

❶ Buckingham Road
❷ Oliver Road
❸ A112 High Road Leyton
❹ Leyton Tube Station (1/4 mile)
❺ Brisbane Road
❻ Windsor Road
❼ Leyton Midland Road BR station
❽ South Stand

Above: 685578; *Right:* 685572

A season of considerable progress on the field — mind you it would have been difficult not to improve on the dire season in 1999/2000 — saw Orient under Tommy Taylor prosper in the Third Division and ultimately grab fifth spot and a place in the Play-Offs. Victory against Hull City saw the side face Blackpool at the Millennium Stadium for the right to play Second Division football in 2001/02. However, in a dramatic game, the Seasiders eventually overcame Orient 4-2, thus consigning the Brisbane Road faithful to another season of Third Division fare. However, the team will undoubtedly start the new campaign as one of the favourites for promotion.

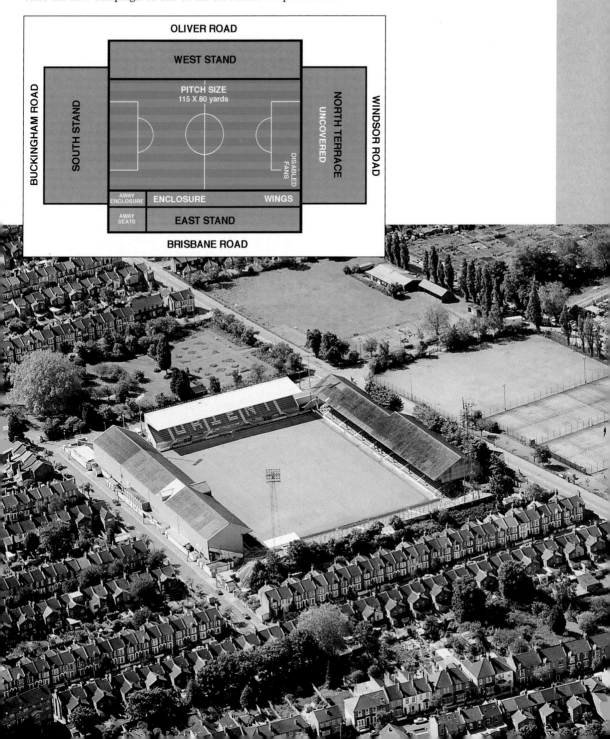

LINCOLN CITY

Sincil Bank, Lincoln, LN5 8LD

Tel No: 01522 880011
Advance Tickets Tel No: 01522 880011
Fax: 01522 880020
Web Site: www.redimps.com
E-Mail: lcfc@redimps.com
League: 3rd Division
Brief History: Founded 1884. Former Ground: John O'Gaunts Ground, moved to Sincil Bank in 1895. Founder-members 2nd Division Football League (1892). Relegated from 4th Division in 1987, promoted from GM Vauxhall Conference in 1988. Record attendance 23,196
(Total) Current Capacity: 10,060 (all seated)
Visiting Supporters' Allocation: 1,934 in Stacey West Stand (now all seated)

Club Colours: Red and white striped shirts, black shorts
Nearest Railway Station: Lincoln Central
Parking (Car): City centre car parks; limited on-street parking
Parking (Coach/Bus): South Common
Police Force and Tel No: Lincolnshire (01522 529911)
Disabled Visitors' Facilities:
  Wheelchairs: The Simons and South (Mundy) Park stands
  Blind: No special facility
Anticipated Development(s): Following the replacement of the seats in the Stacey West Stand, Sincil Bank is once again an all-seater stadium.

KEY
C Club Offices
S Club Shop

↑ North direction (approx)

❶ A46 High Street
❷ Sincil Bank
❸ Sausthorpe Street
❹ Cross Street
❺ Linpave Stand
❻ A158 South Park Avenue
❼ Stacey West Stand (away)
❽ Lincoln Central BR Station (1/2 mile)
❾ Family Stand

Above: 684973; *Right:* 684974

A rocky season for the Imps saw the Sincil Bank team hovering in and around the relegation zone for the duration of the season. The poor form during the course of the season led to the departure of manager Phil Stant in February and his replacement by the experienced Alan Buckley. However, it was off the field where the major change occurred; shortly before Stant's dismissal, the club was bought by the fans and reconstructed as an Industrial & Friendly Society. It will be interesting to see how this change progresses over the years; it may well be ideal when the club remains in the Third Division but for ambition — which in the modern game requires huge finance — it may not be the most appropriate structure. Only time will tell, however, and for 2001/02 fans can probably expect another struggle to retain Nationwide League status.

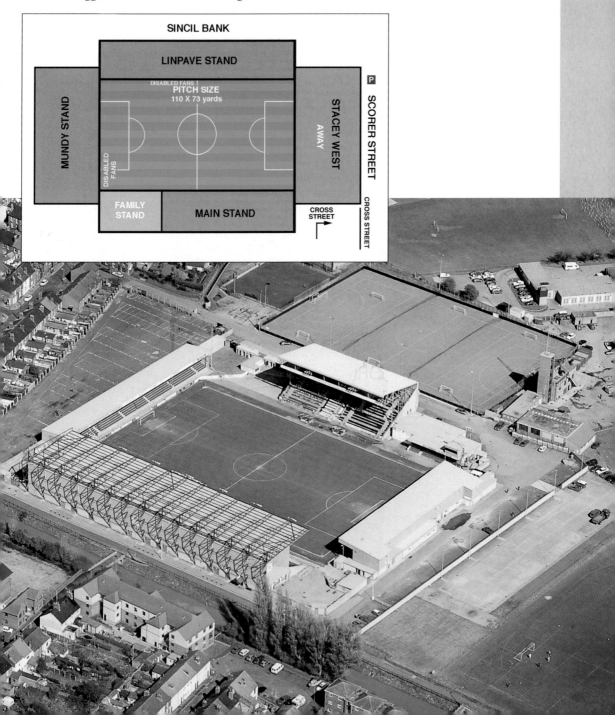

LIVERPOOL

Anfield Road, Liverpool, L4 0TH

Tel No: 0151 263 2361
Advance Tickets Tel No: 0151 260 8680/
   0151 260 9999
Ticket Enquiries Fax: 0151 261 1416
Web Site: http:\\www.liverpoolfc.net
Fax: 0151 260 8813
League: F.A. Premier
Brief History: Founded 1892. Anfield Ground
   formerly Everton F.C. Ground. Joined Football
   League in 1893. Record attendance 61,905
(Total) Current Capacity: 45,362 (all seated)
Visiting Supporters' Allocation: 1,972 (all
   seated) in Anfield Road End
Club Colours: Red shirts, red shorts
Nearest Railway Station: Kirkdale
Parking (Car): Stanley car park
Parking (Coach/Bus): Priory Road and
   Pinehurst Avenue

Police Force and Tel No: Merseyside (0151
   709 6010)
Disabled Visitors' Facilities:
   Wheelchairs: Kop and Main Stands
   Blind: Commentary available
Anticipated Development(s): After examining
   the possibility of expanding Anfield, the club
   has decided to explore the possibility of
   building a new 70,000 stadium costing £150
   million on land about 200yd from Anfield
   adjacent to Stanley Park. If the project
   proceeds, after consultation with the council
   and local residents, it is hoped that the new
   ground will be open for the start of the
   2003/04 season.

KEY

C Club Offices
S Club Shop

↑ North direction (approx)

❶ Car Park
❷ Anfield Road
❸ A5089 Walton Breck Road
❹ Kemlyn Road
❺ Kirkdale BR Station (1 mile)
❻ Utting Avenue
❼ Stanley Park
❽ Spion Kop
❾ Anfield Road Stand

Was 2000/01 the season in which Liverpool finally began to regain its status as one of the great club sides of Europe? Three cups — the Worthington, the FA and the UEFA — as well as a place in the Champions League for 2001/02 all tend to suggest that Gerard Houllier's team is back with a vengeance. With proven goal scorers in Owen and Fowler and with a strong defence and midfield, with England newcomer Stephen Gerrard shining (when fit), everything points to the Reds making a strong challenge for the Premiership in the new campaign. Arguably, however, it was the acquisition of Gary McAllister — surely the purchase of the season — that seemed to be the driving force behind Liverpool's success and as McAllister himself admitted, he can hardly be seen as the future. With two cups to defend and the potential for long campaigns in both the Premiership and the Champions League, much will depend on the depth of Houllier's squad and the ability of many of his injury-prone players to compete week in, week out.

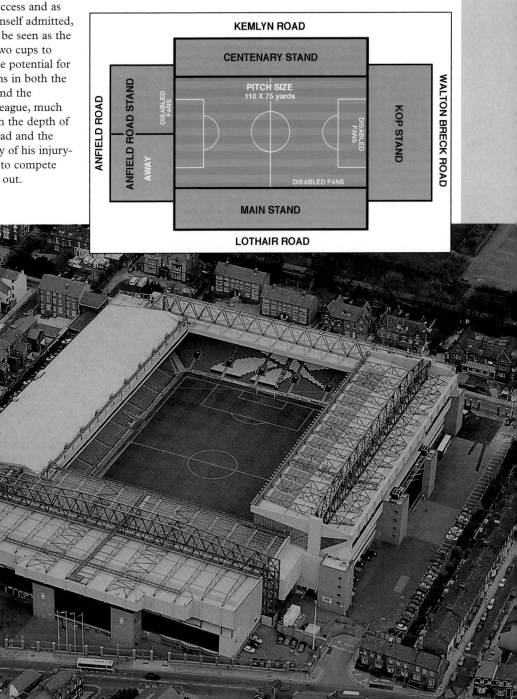

KEMLYN ROAD

CENTENARY STAND

ANFIELD ROAD

ANFIELD ROAD STAND

AWAY

DISABLED FANS

PITCH SIZE
110 X 75 yards

DISABLED FANS

DISABLED FANS

KOP STAND

WALTON BRECK ROAD

MAIN STAND

LOTHAIR ROAD

LUTON TOWN

Kenilworth Road Stadium, 1 Maple Road, Luton, LU4 8AW

Tel No: 01582 411622
Advance Tickets Tel No: 01582 416976
Fax: 01582 405070
Web Site: www.lutontown.co.uk
League: 3rd Division
Brief History: Founded 1885 from an amalgamation of Wanderers F.C. and Excelsior F.C. Former Grounds: Dallow Lane & Dunstable Road, moved to Kenilworth Road in 1905. Record attendance 30,069
(Total) Current Capacity: 9,970 (all seated)
Visiting Supporters' Allocation: 2,200
Club Colours: Orange and blue shirts, blue shorts
Nearest Railway Station: Luton
Parking (Car): Street parking

Parking (Coach/Bus): Luton bus station
Police Force and Tel No: Bedfordshire (01582 401212)
Disabled Visitors' Facilities:
  Wheelchairs: Kenilworth Road
  Blind: Commentary available
Anticipated Development(s): It was announced in February that the club had acquired 55 acres adjacent to Junction 10 on the M1 as the site for the proposed relocation but that any scheme was subject to planning permission being granted. There is, however, no confirmed time scale as to when any development may take place.

KEY	
C	Club Offices
S	Club Shop
E	Entrance(s) for visiting supporters
R	Refreshment bars for visiting supporters
T	Toilets for visiting supporters

⬆ North direction (approx)

❶ To M1 Junction 11
❷ Wimborne Road
❸ Kenilworth Road
❹ Oak Road
❺ Dunstable Road
❻ Luton BR Station (1 mile)
❼ Ticket Office

One of a number of clubs that went through several managers during the course of the season, the Hatters ended the season with former Wimbledon supremo Joe Kinnear at the helm. He had earlier sought to assist Oxford United in their doomed campaign to ensure Second Division survival and, by the time that he replaced Luc Fucillo as manager (he had previously been Director of Football), the team was already struggling to avoid the drop. In the event, Kinnear's undoubted skills were unable to save the Hatters and the club was relegated some dozen points below the safety mark.

MACCLESFIELD TOWN

Moss Rose Ground, London Road, Macclesfield, SK11 7SP

Tel No: 01625 264686
Advance Tickets Tel No: 01625 264686
Fax: 01625 264692
Web Site: http://www.mtfc.co.uk/
E-Mail: webmaster@mtfc.co.uk
League: 3rd Division
Brief History: Founded 1874. Previous ground: Rostron Field moved to Moss Rose Ground in 1891. Winners of the Vauxhall Conference in 1994/95 and 1997/97. Admitted to Football League for 1997/98 season. Record attendance 9,003
(Total) Current Capacity: 6,307 (2,561 seated)
Visiting Supporters' Allocation: 2,127 (1,500 in Silkman Terrace; 627 seated in Estate Road Stand)
Club Colours: Royal blue, royal blue shorts
Nearest Railway Station: Macclesfield
Parking (Car): No parking at the ground and the nearest off-street car park is in the town centre (25min walk). There is some on-street parking in the vicinity, but this can get crowded.
Parking (Coach/Bus): As directed
Police Force and Tel No: Cheshire (01625 610000)
Disabled Visitors' Facilities:
Wheelchairs: Limited facilities
Blind: No special facility
Anticipated Development(s): The new Estate Road (Alfred McAlpine) Stand, with its 1,497 seats, was completed towards the end of the season and officially opened on 5 May 2001. This is the first phase of a scheme to redevelop Moss Rose; the next phase will see a seated second tier raised above the existing terrace at the Silkman End. Other recent work has included the provision of permanent toilets at the away end.

KEY

C Club Offices
E Entrance(s) for visiting supporters

⬆ North direction (approx)

❶ A523 London Road
❷ To Town Centre and BR station (1.5 miles)
❸ To Leek
❹ Moss Lane
❺ Star Lane
❻ Silkmans Public House (now closed)
❼ Star Lane End
❽ Silkman End (away section)
❾ Estate Road Stand

Above: 688550; *Right:* 688570

Since the departure of Sammy McIlroy, the inspirational manager who brought the Silkmen into the Nationwide League and then gained them promotion to the Second Division, Town have floundered back in the Third Division. A further season of lacklustre form saw the team consigned to a position of mid-table mediocrity and cost manager Peter Davenport his job just before the New Year.

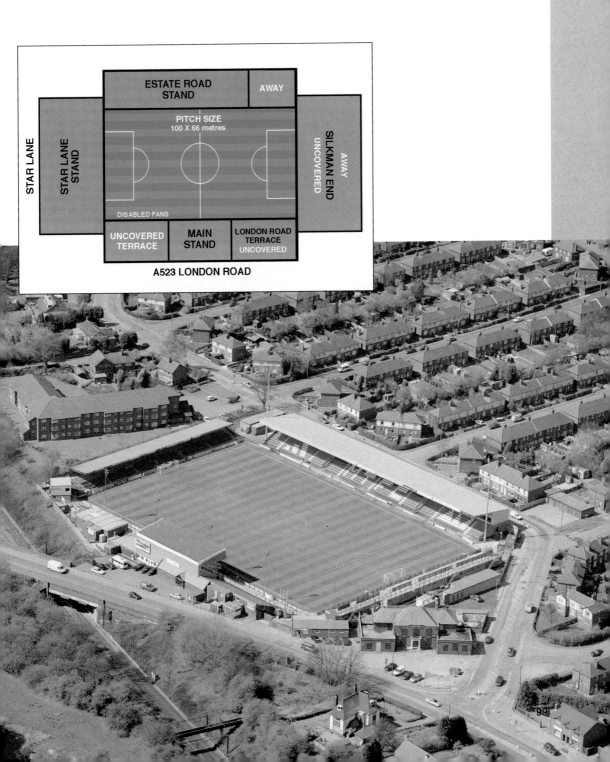

MANCHESTER CITY

Maine Road, Moss Side, Manchester, M14 7WN

Tel No: 0161 232 3000
Advance Tickets Tel No: 0161 226 2224
Fax: 0161 232 8999
E-Mail: mcfc@mcfc.co.uk
Web Site: http://www.mcfc.co.uk
League: 1st Division
Brief History: Founded 1880 as West Gorton, changed name to Ardwick (reformed 1887) and to Manchester City in 1894. Former grounds: Clowes Street, Kirkmanshulme Cricket Club, Donkey Common, Pink Bank Lane & Hyde Road, moved to Maine Road in 1923. Founder-members 2nd Division (1892). Record attendance 84,569 (record for Football League ground)
(Total) Current Capacity: 32,147 (all seated)
Visiting Supporters' Allocation: 3,200
Club Colours: Sky blue shirts, white shorts

Nearest Railway Station: Manchester Piccadilly (2½ miles)
Parking (Car): Street parking and local schools
Parking (Coach/Bus): Kippax Street car park
Police Force and Tel No: Greater Manchester (0161 872 5050)
Disabled Visitors' Facilities:
Wheelchairs: Platt Lane Stand/Kippax Stand
Blind: Main Stand 'G' Block
Anticipated Development(s): The plans for the club to move into the new Millennium Stadium, after the completion of the Commonwealth Games of 2002, are progressing. The current intention is that the club will move to the new stadium, with its planned 50,000 capacity, for the start of the 2003/04 season.

KEY

C Club Offices
S Club Shop
E Entrance(s) for visiting supporters

⬆ North direction (approx)

❶ Thornton Road
❷ South Upper Lloyd Street
❸ To A5103 Princess Road
❹ To City Centre and Manchester Piccadilly BR Station (2½ miles)
❺ To A6010 & M31 Junction 7
❻ Maine Road
❼ Kippax Stand
❽ Main Stand
❾ Platt Lane Stand

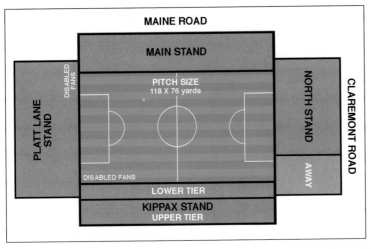

MAINE ROAD

MAIN STAND

PITCH SIZE
118 X 76 yards

DISABLED FANS

PLATT LANE STAND

DISABLED FANS

NORTH STAND

CLAREMONT ROAD

AWAY

LOWER TIER

KIPPAX STAND
UPPER TIER

Like Watford before them, Manchester City discovered that two successive promotions formed no sort of strong platform to achieve Premiership survival, although to do Joe Royle's team of battlers credit, their relegation was not confirmed until the last few games of the season. During the course of the season there were some impressive results — most notably a one-all draw with arch rivals United at Old Trafford — but the team's inconsistency (and a mid-season run of six straight defeats) meant that First Division beckoned. Royle was also not helped by the fact that several of his high profile signings — most notably George Weah — didn't fit in and seemed ill-suited to the type of struggle that City faced. However, City return to the First Division as probably a stronger unit than when they left it in 1999/2000 and, like Charlton before them, should make a strong pitch for one of the automatic promotion spots come May 2002. The new season will, however, start with a new man in the Maine Road hot seat, Kevin Keegan being appointed to replace the sacked Joe Royle.

MANCHESTER UNITED

Old Trafford, Sir Matt Busby Way, Manchester, M16 0RA

Tel No: 0161 868 8000
Advance Tickets Tel No: 0161 868 8020
Fax: 0161 876 5502
Web Site: www.manutd.com
E-mail: webmaster@office.manutd.com
League: F.A. Premier
Brief History: Founded in 1878 as 'Newton Heath L&Y', later Newton Heath, changed to Manchester United in 1902. Former Grounds: North Road, Monsall & Bank Street, Clayton, moved to Old Trafford in 1910 (used Manchester City F.C. Ground 1941-49). Founder-members Second Division (1892). Record attendance 76,962
(Total) Current Capacity: 67,700 (all seated)
Visiting Supporters' Allocation: Approx. 3,000
Club Colours: Red shirts, white shorts

Nearest Railway Station: At Ground
Parking (Car): Lancashire Cricket Ground and White City
Parking (Coach/Bus): As directed by Police
Police Force and Tel No: Greater Manchester (0161 872 5050)
Disabled Visitors' Facilities:
  Wheelchairs: South East Stand
  Blind: Commentary available
Anticipated Development(s): With the completion of the second tiers on both the East and West stands, taking the ground's capacity to 67,000, future work will focus on the construction of a second tier on the South Stand in order to take the ground's capacity to 80,000.

KEY

C Club Offices
S Club Shop

⬆ North direction (approx)

❶ To A5081 Trafford Park Road to M63 Junction 4 (5 miles)
❷ A56 Chester Road
❸ Manchester Ship Canal
❹ To Old Trafford Cricket Ground
❺ To Parking and Warwick Road BR Station
❻ Sir Matt Busby Way

Above: 688593; Right: 688583

If winning the championship alone can be regarded as a disappointment, then United had a highly disappointing season. Knocked out of the FA Cup by an almost surreal goal from West Ham United — it's nice to see that in Fabien Barthez United retains its uncanny ability to field eccentric goalkeepers — and out of the Champions League by Bayern Munich, United's premature (and relatively easy) retention of the Premiership was something of an anticlimax. Given that United wish to be measured in European if not global terms, their failure to convert domestic dominance into European glory must rankle both with the management and with the fans. The new season marks Alex Ferguson's last in charge at Old Trafford and probably the end of an era; new signings are certain to appear during the summer — of which van Nistelrooy is the first — and some of the old guard may well move on. Fergie would no doubt like to go out on a high; one suspects that his heart is set on one final European triumph and that the domestic game has perhaps lost its challenge. United will certainly be the favourites for the Premiership, but 2001/02 could see the title going right to the wire.

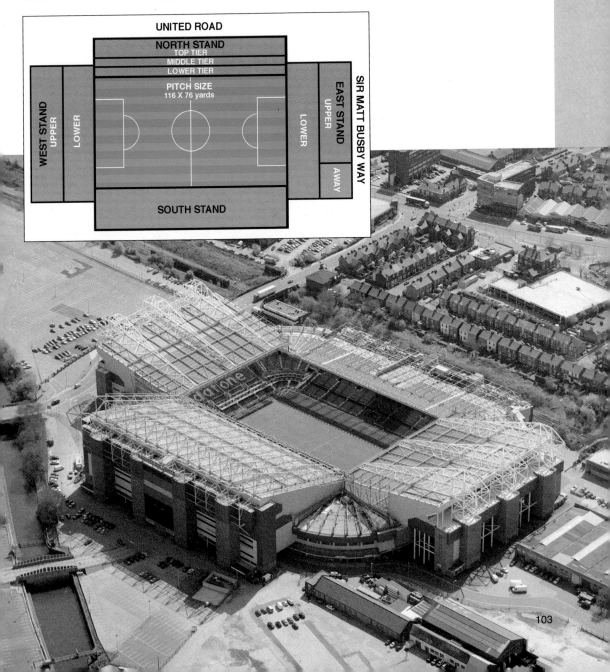

MANSFIELD TOWN

Field Mill Ground, Quarry Lane, Mansfield, Notts, NG18 5DA

Tel No: 01623 482482
Advance Tickets Tel No: 01623 482483
Fax: 01623 482195
Web Site: www.mansfieldtown.net
E-mail: info@mansfieldtown.net
League: 3rd Division
Brief History: Founded 1910 as Mansfield Wesleyans Boys Brigade, changed to Mansfield Town in 1914. Former Grounds: Pelham Street, Newgate Lane and The Prairie, moved to Field Mill in 1919. Record attendance 24,467
(Total) Current Capacity: 9,990 (all seated)
Visiting Supporters' Allocation: 1,983 (all seated) in South Stand
Club Colours: Amber with blue trim shirts, Amber shorts with blue trim

Nearest Railway Station: Mansfield
Parking (Car): Car park at Ground
Parking (Coach/Bus): Car park at Ground
Police Force and Tel No: Nottinghamshire (01623 420999)
Disabled Visitors' Facilities:
  Wheelchairs: Facilities provided in North, West and South (away) stands
  Blind: No special facility
Anticipated Development(s): Work on the Main Stand and on the North and Quarry Lane ends was completed in early 2001 and work will commence in the reconstruction of the Bishop Street Stand during the 2001/02 season.

KEY

E Entrance(s) for visiting supporters

R Refreshment bars for visiting supporters

T Toilets for visiting supporters

↑ North direction (approx)

❶ Car Park
❷ Quarry Lane
❸ A60 Nottingham Road to M1 Junction 27
❹ Portland Street
❺ To A38 and M1 Junction 28
❻ To Town Centre
❼ Mansfield railway station
❽ North Stand
❾ Quarry Lane End (South Stand)
❿ Bishop Street Stand
⓫ Main (West) Stand

Above: 687960; *Right:* 687954

Dramatic progress off the field, with the reconstruction of Field Mill proceeding apace, was matched by limited progress on it. Under Billy Dearden, the club moved slightly closer to the Play-Offs, finishing 12th in 2000/01 as opposed to 17th in the previous season. Once Field Mill is completed, it will represent one of the few all-seater grounds in the lower divisions; fans will be hoping that the team can improve sufficiently to match the facilities.

MIDDLESBROUGH

BT Cellnet Riverside Stadium, Middlesbrough, Cleveland

Tel No: 01642 877700
Advance Tickets Tel No: 01642 877745
Fax: 01642 877840
Web Site: www.mfc.co.uk
E-mail: pr-dept@mfc.co.uk
League: F.A. Premiership
Brief History: Founded 1876. Former Grounds: Archery Ground (Albert Park), Breckon Hill Road, Linthorpe Road, moved to Ayresome Park in 1903, and to current ground in Summer 1995. F.A. Amateur Cup winners 1894 and 1897 (joined Football League in 1899). Record attendance (Ayresome Park) 53,596, (Riverside Stadium) 34,800
(Total) Current Capacity: 35,100 (all seated)
Visiting Supporters' Allocation: 3,450 (in the South Stand)

Club Colours: Red and white shirts, white shorts
Nearest Railway Station: Middlesbrough
Parking (Car): All parking at stadium is for permit holders
Parking (Coach/Bus): As directed
Police Force and Tel No: Cleveland (01642 248184)
Disabled Visitors' Facilities:
Wheelchairs: More than 360 places available for disabled fans
Blind: Commentary available
Anticipated Development(s): There remain long term plans for the ground's capacity to be increased to 42,000 through the construction of extra tiers on the North, South and East stands, although there is no confirmed timetable for this work at the current time.

KEY

C Club Offices
S Club Shop

↑ North direction (approx)

❶ Cargo Fleet Road
❷ Middlesbrough station
❸ Middlesbrough town centre
❹ Middlesbrough Docks (1 mile) and Town Centre
❺ A66
❻ Borough Road
❼ Car Park
❽ South Stand

For much of the season it looked as though Boro was doomed and that Brian Robson's expensive squad would be facing relegation to the First Division, despite all the investment from chairman Steve Gibson in ground and players. The dire situation faced was brought home by the fact that Boro was outplayed at home by Bradford City and required a last minute equaliser to salvage a point; the relief on Robson's face was graphically caught by the press cameras. Defeat for Boro in that game, it was confidently expected, would lead to Robson's departure. In the event, however, Terry Venables was persuaded to come in as Robson's 'friend and mentor' and the team's results improved significantly. Not assured of retaining Premiership status until the last week of the season, much will depend for Boro in 2001/02 on new manager Steve McClaren, formerly number two at Old Trafford. With McClaren's arrival, it was farewell to Robson and to his coaching staff Viv Anderson and Gordon McQueen as well as to 'El Tel'.

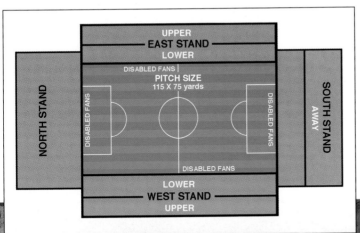

UPPER
EAST STAND
LOWER

NORTH STAND

DISABLED FANS

DISABLED FANS
PITCH SIZE
115 X 75 yards

DISABLED FANS

DISABLED FANS

SOUTH STAND
AWAY

LOWER
WEST STAND
UPPER

MILLWALL

New Den, Bolina Road, London, SE16 3LN

Tel No: 020 7232 1222
Advance Tickets Tel No: 020 7231 9999
Fax: 020 7231 3663
Web Site: www.millwallfc.co.uk
League: 1st Division
Brief History: Founded 1885 as Millwall Rovers, changed name to Millwall Athletic (1889) and Millwall (1925). Former Grounds: Glengall Road, East Ferry Road (2 separate Grounds), North Greenwich Ground and The Den – Cold Blow Lane – moved to New Den 1993/94 season. Founder-members Third Division (1920). Record attendance (at The Den) 48,672 (at New Den) 20,093

(Total) Current Capacity: 20,150 (all seated)
Visiting Supporters' Allocation: 4,382
Club Colours: White shirts, silver shorts
Nearest Railway Station: South Bermondsey or Surrey Docks (Tube)
Parking (Car): Juno Way car parking (8 mins walk)
Parking (Coach/Bus): At Ground
Police Force and Tel No: Metropolitan (0171 679 9217)
Disabled Visitors' Facilities:
  Wheelchairs: 200 spaces in West Stand Lower Tier
  Blind: Commentary available

KEY

C Club Offices
S Club Shop
E Entrance(s) for visiting supporters

↑ North direction (approx)

❶ Bolina Road
❷ South Bermondsey BR
❸ Surrey Quays Underground
❹ Zampa Road
❺ Ilderton Road
❻ To Rotherhithe New Road and Rotherhithe Tunnel
❼ To New Cross
❽ Surrey Canal Road

For once the Lions roared and under Mark McGhee, Millwall proved the pre-season pundits correct and went several stages better than in the previous two seasons by not only gaining automatic promotion but also, courtesy of results on the last Saturday (when Millwall thrashed Oldham at home and Rotherham were hold to a draw), came away with the Second Division championship as well. In one of the two automatic promotion spots for virtually the full season, their position at the top was only threatened by Rotherham and, until the late stages of the season, by Reading. The new season will bring First Division football to the New Den. The club has the potential to thrive at this higher level but as always the first season for any promoted team may be a struggle.

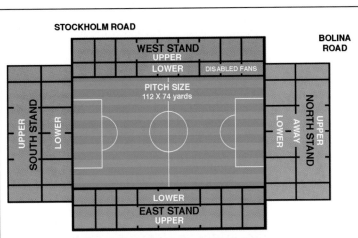

STOCKHOLM ROAD

BOLINA ROAD

WEST STAND
UPPER
LOWER   DISABLED FANS

PITCH SIZE
112 X 74 yards

UPPER
SOUTH STAND

LOWER

UPPER
NORTH STAND
AWAY
LOWER

LOWER
EAST STAND
UPPER

NEWCASTLE UNITED

St. James' Park, Newcastle-upon-Tyne, NE1 4ST

Tel No: 0191 201 8400
Advance Tickets Tel No: 0191 261 1571
Fax: 0191 201 8600
Web Site: www.nufc.co.uk
E-mail: admin@nufc.co.uk
League: F.A. Premier
Brief History: Founded in 1882 as Newcastle East End, changed to Newcastle United in 1892. Former Grounds: Chillingham Road, moved to St. James' Park (former home of defunct Newcastle West End) in 1892. Record attendance 68,386
(Total) Current Capacity: 52,000 (all seated)
Visiting Supporters' Allocation: 3,000 in North East Stand
Club Colours: Black and white striped shirts, black shorts

Nearest Railway Station: Newcastle Central
Parking (Car): Leazes car park and street parking
Parking (Coach/Bus): Leazes car park
Police Force and Tel No: Northumbria (0191 232 3451)
Disabled Visitors' Facilities:
Wheelchairs: 103 spaces available
Blind: Commentary available
Anticipated Development(s): With work now completed on both the enlarged Millburn and Sir John Hall stands, the capacity at St James' Park is now about 52,000. Further redevelopment at the ground is, however, problematic given the lie of the land on the north side, and the club has no immediate plans for further work once the current programme is completed.

KEY

C Club Offices
S Club Shop

↑ North direction (approx)

❶ St. James's Park
❷ Strawberry Place
❸ Gallowgate
❹ Away Section
❺ To Newcastle Central BR Station (¹/₂ mile) & A6127(M)
❻ Car Park
❼ Barrack Road (A189)
❽ To A1 and North
❾ Corporation Street
❿ Percy Road
⓫ Metro Station

Above: 687972; *Right:* 687965

A disappointing season for the Magpies culminated in the team achieving a position of mid-table mediocrity (or security depending on how it is viewed). Undoubtedly Bobby Robson possesses a talented squad with youthfulness — players Kieron Dyer — allied to guile and experience — represented by Alan Shearer, but somehow the total seems to be less than the sum of the parts and a number of lacklustre performances — such as the 3-0 defeat by Liverpool (marked by a Michael Owen hat-trick) — will no doubt mean that Robson will be thinking further about his squad. But there are rumours that Dyer may be a big money transfer away from St James' Park and, with Alan Shearer now spending more time on the treatment table than on the pitch, unless the purse strings are loosened, United might be one of the candidates for relegation. Expect some well chewed fingernails on Tyneside come April/May 2002.

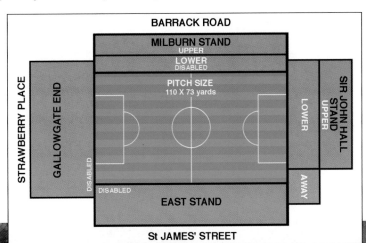

NORTHAMPTON TOWN

Sixfields Stadium, Northampton, NN5 5QA

Tel No: 0870 011 7773
Advance Tickets Tel No: 0870 011 7773
Fax: 0870 011 7774
Web Site: www.ntfc.co.uk
League: 2nd Division
Brief History: Founded 1897. Former, County, Ground was part of Northamptonshire County Cricket Ground. Moved to Sixfields Stadium during early 1994/95 season. Record attendance 24,523 (at County Ground); 7,557 (at Sixfields)
(Total) Current Capacity: 7,653 (all seated)

Visiting Supporters' Allocation: 1,277 (all seated)
Club Colours: Claret with white sleeved shirts, white shorts
Nearest Railway Station: Northampton Castle
Parking (Car): Adjacent to Ground
Parking (Coach/Bus): Adjacent to Ground
Police Force and Tel No: Northants (01604 700700)
Disabled Visitors' Facilities:
  Wheelchairs: Available on all four sides
  Blind: Available

KEY

C Club Offices
S Club Shop
E Entrance(s) for visiting supporters
R Refreshment bars for visiting supporters
T Toilets for visiting supporters

⬆ North direction (approx)

❶ South Stand (away)
❷ Athletics Stand
❸ To Upton Way roundabout (A45) with connections to Northampton Town Centre and M1 (North) and M1 (South)
❹ Car parks

Above: 688614; Right: 688605

Promoted at the end of 2000/01, the Cobblers were inevitably one of the pre-season favourites to make the quick return to the Third Division. In the event, however, the team managed to stay just above the relegation dogfight and finish in 18th place some six points clear of the drop zone, despite a 3-0 drubbing by Walsall in the last game of the season. However, with a number of ambitious teams coming up from the Third Division, the battle to avoid the drop in 2001/02 may well be harder than that last year and the team will need to perform to its peak in order to retain its Second Division status. With Rushden & Diamonds having – finally – achieved Nationwide League status, there will be an interesting couple of years in Northamptonshire to see which team emerges as top dog.

NORWICH CITY

Carrow Road, Norwich, NR1 1JE

Tel No: 01603 760760
Advance Tickets Tel No: 01603 761661
Fax: 01603 613886
Web Site: www.canaries.co.uk
E-Mail: reception@ncfc-canaries.co.uk
League: 1st Division
Brief History: Founded 1902. Former grounds: Newmarket Road and the Nest, Rosary Road; moved to Carrow Road in 1935. Founder-members 3rd Division (1920). Record attendance 43,984
(Total) Current Capacity: 21,414 (seated)
Visiting Supporters' Allocation: 1,741 (South Stand Blocks F, G, H)

Club Colours: Yellow with green side panel shirts, green shorts
Nearest Railway Station: Norwich
Parking (Car): City centre car parks
Parking (Coach/Bus): Lower Clarence Road
Police Force and Tel No: Norfolk (01603 621212)
Disabled Visitors' Facilities:
  Wheelchairs: South Stand (heated)
  Blind: Commentary available
Anticipated Development(s): The next stage in the redevelopment of Carrow Road will involve the reconstruction of the South Stand, but there is as yet no timescale for this work.

KEY

C Club Offices
S Club Shop
E Entrance(s) for visiting supporters

↑ North direction (approx)

❶ Carrow Road
❷ A47 King Street
❸ River Wensum
❹ Riverside
❺ Car Park
❻ Norwich BR Station

Another season of mediocrity for City — made all the more galling by the plaudits given to local rivals Ipswich Town — resulted in a worse position than that achieved in 1999/2000, with the club hovering just above the relegation zone. Bryan Hamilton's tenure in the Carrow Road hot seat proved to be short-lived; he was sacked barely half way through his first season, with Nigel Worthington being appointed his successor. Whilst Ipswich Town can look forward to European football in 2001/02, City are consigned again to games at Grimsby and Crewe — a far cry from the club's own European exploits.

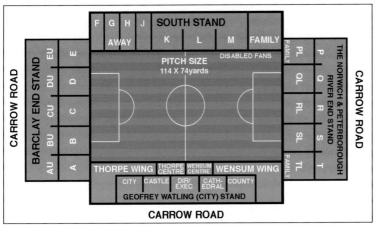

NOTTINGHAM FOREST

City Ground, Nottingham, NG2 5FJ

Tel No: 0115 982 4444
Advance Tickets Tel No: 0115 982 4445
Fax: 0115 982 4455
Web Site: http://www.nottinghamforest.co.uk
E-Mail: info@nottinghamforest.co.uk
League: 1st Division
Brief History: Founded 1865 as Forest Football Club, changed name to Nottingham Forest (c1879). Former Grounds: Forest Recreation Ground, Meadow Cricket Ground, Trent Bridge (Cricket Ground), Parkside, Gregory Ground and Town Ground, moved to City Ground in 1898. Founder-members of Second Division (1892). Record attendance 49,945

(Total) Current Capacity: 30,602 (all seated)
Visiting Supporters' Allocation: Approx 4,750
Club Colours: Red shirts, white shorts
Nearest Railway Station: Nottingham Midland
Parking (Car): East car park and street parking
Parking (Coach/Bus): East car park
Police Force and Tel No: Nottinghamshire (0115 948 1888)
Disabled Visitors' Facilities:
  Wheelchairs: Front of Executive Stand
  Blind: No special facility

KEY

C Club Offices
S Club Shop
E Entrance(s) for visiting supporters

↑ North direction (approx)

❶ Radcliffe Road
❷ Lady Bay Bridge Road
❸ Trent Bridge
❹ Trent Bridge Cricket Ground
❺ Notts County F.C.
❻ River Trent
❼ Nottingham Midland BR Station (1/2 mile)

Following the disappointment of David Platt's first season at the City Ground, when the team had struggled at the wrong end of the First Division, 2000/01 saw a distinct improvement in the club's fortunes with a Play-Off position a distinct possibility. However, the team was unable to bridge the gap and finished in 11th place. With the Premiership 'parachute' now expired, the team will face increasing pressure from the other 'fallen giants' of the English game if Forest are going to reclaim their position in the Premiership. The challenge of 2001/02 will be faced by a new manager – Paul Hart – who was appointed when Platt departed to join the England set-up.

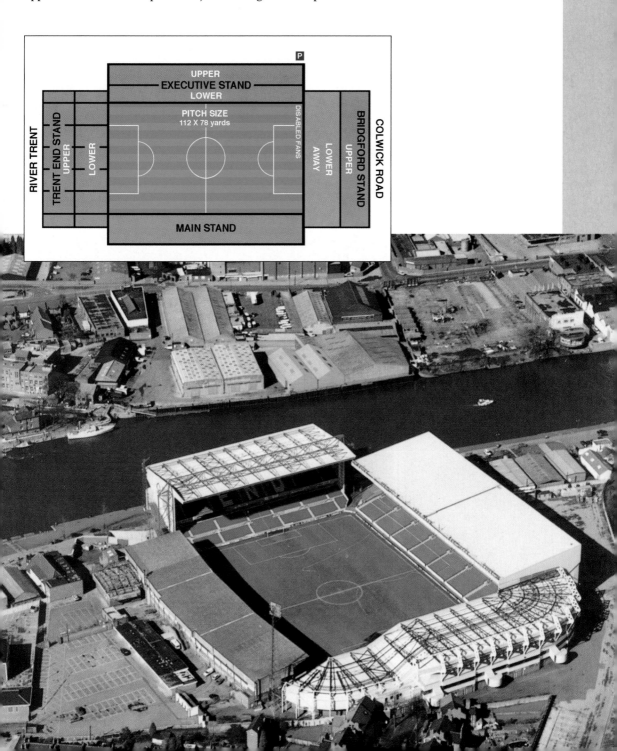

UPPER
EXECUTIVE STAND
LOWER

PITCH SIZE
112 X 78 yards

RIVER TRENT

TRENT END STAND

UPPER

LOWER

DISABLED FANS

LOWER
AWAY

UPPER

BRIDGFORD STAND

COLWICK ROAD

MAIN STAND

NOTTS COUNTY

Meadow Lane, Nottingham, NG2 3HJ

Tel No: 0115 952 9000
Advance Tickets Tel No: 0115 955 7210
Fax: 0115 955 3994
Web Site: www.nottscountyfc.co.uk
E-Mail: info@nottscountyfc.co.uk
League: 2nd Division
Brief History: Founded 1862 (oldest club in Football League) as Nottingham, changed to Notts County in c1882. Former Grounds: Notts Cricket Ground (Beeston), Castle Cricket Ground, Trent Bridge Cricket Ground, moved to Meadow Lane in 1910. Founder-members Football League (1888). Record attendance 47,310

(Total) Current Capacity: 20,300 (seated)
Visiting Supporters' Allocation: 5,438 (seated)
Club Colours: Black and white striped shirts, black shorts
Nearest Railway Station: Nottingham Midland
Parking (Car): Mainly street parking
Parking (Coach/Bus): Cattle market
Police Force and Tel No: Nottingham (0115 948 1888)
Disabled Visitors' Facilities:
  Wheelchairs: Meadow Lane/Jimmy Sirrel/Derek Pavis Stands
  Blind: No special facility

KEY

C Club Offices
S Club Shop
E Entrance(s) for visiting supporters
R Refreshment bars for visiting supporters
T Toilets for visiting supporters

↑ North direction (approx)

❶ A6011 Meadow Lane
❷ County Road
❸ A60 London Road
❹ River Trent
❺ Nottingham Midland BR Station (½ mile)

Having finished in eighth place at the end of 1999/2000, Jocky Scott's team showed remarkable consistency in 2000/01 and again finished in eighth place, although the difference in points between County's position and sixth was reduced to only six points (from the 15 of the previous season). If the club can continue in a similar vein in 2001/02 then a Play-Off position will become a very real possibility at Meadow Lane.

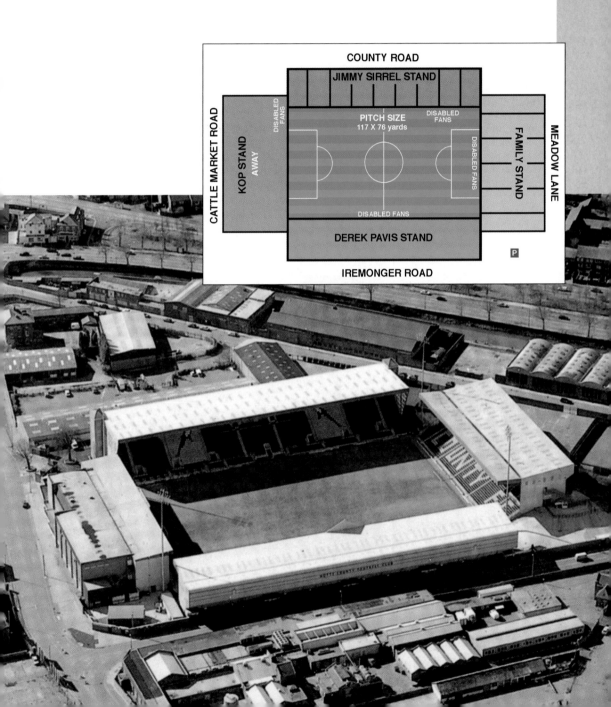

OLDHAM ATHLETIC

Boundary Park, Oldham, OL1 2PA

Tel No: 0161 624 4972
Advance Tickets Tel No: 0161 624 4972
Fax: 0161 627 5915
Web Site: www.oldhamathletic.co.uk
League: 2nd Division
Brief History: Founded 1897 as Pine Villa,
changed name to Oldham Athletic in 1899.
Former Grounds: Berry's Field, Pine Mill,
Athletic Ground (later named Boundary Park),
Hudson Fold, moved to Boundary Park in
1906. Record attendance 47,671
(Total) Current Capacity: 13,559 (all seated)
Visiting Supporters' Allocation: 1,800
minimum, 4,600 maximum
Club Colours: Blue shirts, blue shorts
Nearest Railway Station: Oldham Werneth
Parking (Car): Lookers Stand car park

Parking (Coach/Bus): At Ground
Police Force and Tel No: Greater Manchester
(0161 624 0444)
Disabled Visitors' Facilities:
  Wheelchairs: Rochdale Road and Seton Stands
  Blind: No special facility
Anticipated Development(s): The plans for
the construction of a new 15,000-seat ground
at Clayton Playing Fields in conjunction with
the local RLFC club have been abandoned. As
a result, Athletic will now seek to redevelop
Boundary Park further, with the first phase
being the construction of a new two-tier stand,
costing £15 million, to replace the Lookers
Stand. There is, however, no confirmed
timetable for this work at the current time.

KEY

C Club Offices
E Entrance(s) for visiting
supporters

⬆ North direction (approx)

❶ A663 Broadway
❷ Furtherwood Road
❸ Chadderton Way
❹ To A627(M) and M62
❺ To Oldham Werneth BR
Station (1½ miles)
❻ Car Park

Above: 685004; Right: 685008

A further season of struggle at Boundary Park again saw Andy Ritchie's team more concerned with events in the Second Division's basement, but again 15th position — as opposed to the 14th achieved in 1999/2000 — ensures that Second Division football will be on offer to the loyal fans in the new campaign. However, the club has recently changed hands and, whilst it is uncertain at the time of writing what impact this will have, it is almost certain to lead to changes before the launch of the 2001/02 season.

OXFORD UNITED

Kassam Stadium, Grenoble Road, Blackbird Leys, Oxford OX4 4XP

Tel No: 01865 337500
Advance Tickets Tel No: 01865 337533
Fax: 01865 337555
Web Site: www.oufc.co.uk
E-Mail: admin@oufc.co.uk
League: 3rd Division
Brief History: Founded in 1893 as Headington (later Headington United)m changed name to Oxford United in 1960. Former grounds: Britannia Inn Field, Headington Quarry, Wooten's Field, Manor Ground and The Paddocks. The club moved back to the Manor Ground in 1925. Moved — finally — to new ground at Minchery Farm in 2001. Record attendance (at the Manor Ground) 22,730.
(Total) Current Capacity: 12,500
Visiting Supporters' Allocation: c5,000 in North Stand
Club Colours: Yellow with blue trim shirts and navy with yellow trim shorts
Nearest Railway Station: Oxford
Parking (Car): 1,100 spaces at ground
Parking (Coach/Bus): As directed
Police Force and Tel No: Thames Valley (01865 777501)
Disabled Visitors' Facilities:
Wheelchairs: c80 disabled spaces
Blind: No special facility
Anticipated Development(s): With, after many years of struggle, the partial completion of the new £15 million ground at Minchery Farm after something like five years, Oxford United now have much improved facilities. There are plans for the construction of a fourth side to the ground eventually, but much will depend on the club's status.

KEY

↑ North direction (approx)

❶ Grenoble Road
❷ To A4074
❸ Northfield School
❹ To Oxford city centre and railway station (four/five miles respectively)
❺ Blackbird Leys Estate
❻ Knights Road
❼ North Stand
❽ South Stand
❾ East Stand
❿ To B480

Above: 688785; *Right:* 688774

A truly appalling season for the team, saw United rock bottom for the duration thus continuing the free-fall that had marked the 1999/2000 season. Despite the presence of erstwhile Wimbledon manager, Joe Kinnear, for part of the season — he later departed to 'spend more time with his family' before re-emerging as manager of equally doomed Luton Town — he failed to reverse the almost inexorable decline to the Third Division. The team manger, David Kemp, departed before the end of the season; fans will be hoping that the new incumbent will be able to inspire a revival otherwise a one-way trip to the Conference looks a distinct possibility. Having achieving barely a point on average every two games, the club will grace its new ground facing new local rivals in Cheltenham Town — a far cry from only three years ago when the team was a reasonable First Division outfit. New manager Mark Wright will certainly have his work cut out in 2001/02.

PETERBOROUGH UNITED

London Road, Peterborough, Cambs, PE2 8AL

Tel No: 01733 563947
Advance Tickets Tel No: 01733 319863
Fax: 01733 344140
Web Site: www.theposh.com
E-Mail: football@theposh.com
League: 2nd Division
Brief History: Founded in 1934 (no connection with former 'Peterborough and Fletton United' FC). Elected to Football League in 1960. Record attendance 30,096
(Total) Current Capacity: 13,870 (8,048 seated)
Visiting Supporters' Allocation: 3,758 (756 seated)
Club Colours: Blue shirts, white shorts

Nearest Railway Station: Peterborough
Parking (Car): Peterborough
Parking (Coach/Bus): At ground
Police Force and Tel No: Cambridgeshire (01733 563232
Disabled Visitors' Facilities:
  Wheelchairs: South Stand
  Blind: No special facility
Future Development(s): Following the reroofing of the Moys and London Road ends, long term plans exist for the construction of a new Main Stand — for which plans have been prepared — and other work. However, there is no confirmed timetable for this at present.

KEY

C Club Offices
S Club Shop
E Entrance(s) for visiting supporters
R Refreshment bars for visiting supporters
T Toilets for visiting supporters

↑ North direction (approx)

❶ A15 London Road
❷ Car Parks
❸ Peterborough BR Station (1 mile)
❹ Glebe Road
❺ A605
❻ To A1 (north) (5 miles)
❼ River Nene
❽ To Whittlesey
❾ To A1 (south) (5 miles)

Above: 685033; *Right:* 685030

A season of consolidation for Barry Fry and his Posh team, saw Peterborough United cement their Second Division status with a finishing position of 12th. It is not long ago, however, that Peterborough were a Nationwide First Division outfit — for two seasons at least — and at the start of the club's fifth decade in the Football League fans will be ardently hoping that this status can be reacquired.

PLYMOUTH ARGYLE

Home Park, Plymouth, PL2 3DQ

Tel No: 01752 562561
Advance Tickets Tel No: 01752 562561
Fax: 01752 606167
Web-site: www.pafc.co.uk
E-mail: argyle@pafc.co.uk
League: 3rd Division
Brief History: Founded 1886 as Argyle Athletic Club, changed name to Plymouth Argyle in 1903. Founder-members Third Division (1920). Record attendance 43,596
(Total) Current Capacity: 19,589 (7,000 seated) (prior to redevelopment)
Visiting Supporters' Allocation: 1,990 (120 seated) in Barn Park End and Grandstand (Barn Park Wing) (prior to redevelopment)
Club Colours: Green shirts, green shorts
Nearest Railway Station: Plymouth

Parking (Car): Car park adjacent
Parking (Coach/Bus): Central car park
Police Force and Tel No: Devon & Cornwall (01752 701188)
Disabled Visitors' Facilities:
  Wheelchairs: Devonport End
  Blind: Commentary available
Anticipated Development(s): Work started on the redevelopment of the ground in the summer of 2001 (unfortunately after the cut-off date for photography in the book) and involves the demolition of the Barn Park, Devonport and Lyndhurst stands and their replacement by a new horseshoe-shaped all-seater stand accommodating 12,700. Work on this structure should be completed by the end of 2001.

KEY

C Club Offices
S Club Shop
E Entrance(s) for visiting supporters
R Refreshment bars for visiting supporters
T Toilets for visiting supporters

↑ North direction (approx)

❶ Outland Road
❷ Car Park
❸ Devonport Road
❹ Central Park
❺ Town Centre & Plymouth BR Station (½ mile)

With a potentially talented and youthful squad, much was expected from Kevin Hodges's team during 2000/01, with an expectation amongst fans that, to coin a phrase, 'things could only get better' and that 12th at the end of the 1999/2000 season was the foundation for a strong push towards promotion in 2000/01. How wrong can you be? In reality, the team struggled and finishing 13th was a considerable disappointment. With its fan base, Argyle certainly has the potential to be a bigger club;

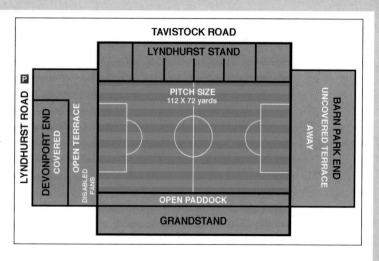

unfortunately, it doesn't seem able to drag itself out of mid-table mediocrity in the Third Division. Expect more of the same in 2001/02.

PORTSMOUTH

Fratton Park, 57 Frogmore Road, Portsmouth, Hants, PO4 8RA

Tel No: 02392 731204
Advance Tickets Tel No: 02392 618777
Fax: 02392 734129
Web Site: www.pompeyfc.co.uk
E-Mail: pfc@portsmouthfc.dbx.co.uk
League: 1st Division
Brief History: Founded 1898. Founder-members Third Division (1920). Record attendance 51,385
(Total) Current Capacity: 19,214 (all seated)
  Visiting Supporters' Allocation: 3,121 (max) in Milton Stand
Club Colours: Blue shirts, white shorts
Nearest Railway Station: Fratton

Parking (Car): Street parking
Parking (Coach/Bus): As directed by Police
Police Force and Tel No: Hampshire (02392 321111)
Disabled Visitors' Facilities:
  Wheelchairs: KJC Stand
  Blind: No special facility
Anticipated Development(s): The club has plans for a new 35,000 all-seater stadium to be called the Pompey Centre and this has received local authority approval, although there is not yet a confirmed schedule for if and when this work will be undertaken.

KEY

- **C** Club Offices
- **S** Club Shop
- **E** Entrance(s) for visiting supporters
- **R** Refreshment bars for visiting supporters
- **T** Toilets for visiting supporters

⬆ North direction (approx)

❶ Alverstone Road
❷ Carisbrook Road
❸ A288 Milton Road
❹ A2030 Velder Avenue A27
❺ A2030 Goldsmith Avenue
❻ Fratton BR station (½ mile)
❼ KJC Stand

It was certainly an eventful season at Fratton Park, with the club going through managers as though they were going out of fashion. Starting the season with Tony Pulis, he was later replaced by Steve Claridge, before he in turn succumbed to the new incumbent Graham Rix. In terms of what happened on the pitch, this might have been incidental except for the fact that the team was heading down the league table and apparently for the Second Division, particularly when in the penultimate game Pompey lost 4-2 at home to fellow strugglers Crystal Palace — a game that the Eagles had to win to ensure that they had any chance of beating the drop. The final relegation spot rested on the last Sunday: Portsmouth duly despatched Barnsley 3-0 at home and results elsewhere meant that Huddersfield Town face the drop. If Rix can build a decent squad, then Pompey ought to be able to sustain a good First Division campaign in 2001/02, but another struggle looks to be on the cards.

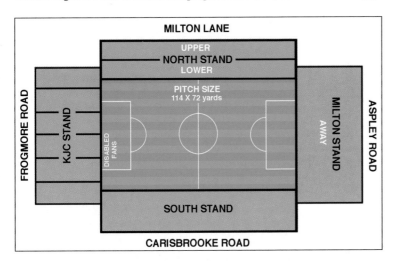

PORT VALE

Vale Park, Burslem, Stoke-on-Trent, ST6 1AW

Tel No: 01782 655800
Advance Tickets Tel No: 01782 811707
Fax: 01782 834981
Web Site: www.portvale.co.uk
E-Mail: pvfc@port-vale.co.uk
League: 2nd Division
Brief History: Founded 1876 as Burslem Port Vale, changed name to 'Port Vale' in 1907 (reformed club). Former Grounds: The Meadows Longport, Moorland Road Athletic Ground, Cobridge Athletic Grounds, Recreation Ground Hanley, moved to Vale Park in 1950. Founder-members Second Division (1892). Record attendance 48,749
(Total) Current Capacity: 23,500 (all seated)
Visiting Supporters' Allocation: 4,550 (in Hamil Road Stand)

Club Colours: White shirts, white shorts
Nearest Railway Station: Longport (two miles)
Parking (Car): Car park at Ground
Parking (Coach/Bus): Hamil Road car park
Police Force and Tel No: Staffordshire (01782 577114)
Disabled Visitors' Facilities:
Wheelchairs: 200 spaces in new Britannic Disabled Stand
Blind: Commentary available
Anticipated Development(s): Completion of the new 5,000-seat Lorne Street marks the end of current plans for the redevelopment of Vale Park.

KEY

C Club Offices
S Club Shop
E Entrance(s) for visiting supporters

⬆ North direction (approx)

❶ Car Parks
❷ Hamil Road
❸ Lorne Street
❹ To B5051 Moorland Road
❺ To Burslem Town Centre
❻ Railway Stand
❼ Sentinel Stand
❽ Hamil Road Stand
❾ Lorne Street Stand (under construction)
❿ Family Section

130

Above: 688624; *Right:* 688620

Relegation back to the Second Division in 1999/2000 ensured that there would be local derbies against Stoke City in 2000/01 and the fact that both Potteries' teams remain in the Second Division for 2001/02 means that the intense local rivalry will continue for at least another season. Under Brian Horton, Vale never really challenged for either promotion or the Play-Offs, although finishing 11th at the end was better than it might have been at one stage of the season and at least provides a useful foundation for a further assault on the Second Division promotion race in 2001/02 when, at the very least, fans will be hoping that the team can reverse the fortunes and ensure a finishing position above Stoke City. One coup, however, was the defeat of Brentford in the LDV Vans trophy at the Millennium Stadium on 22 April which brought much needed silverware to Vale Park.

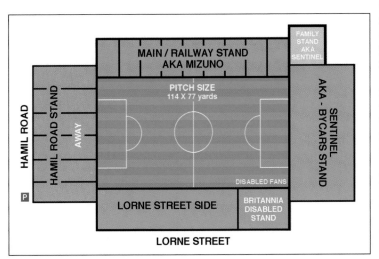

HAMIL ROAD

HAMIL ROAD STAND

AWAY

MAIN / RAILWAY STAND
AKA MIZUNO

FAMILY STAND AKA SENTINEL

PITCH SIZE
114 X 77 yards

SENTINEL AKA - BYCARS STAND

DISABLED FANS

LORNE STREET SIDE

BRITANNIA DISABLED STAND

LORNE STREET

P

PRESTON NORTH END

Deepdale, Sir Tom Finney Way, Preston, PR1 6RU

Tel No: 01772 902020
Advance Tickets Tel No: 01772 902222
Fax: 01772 653266
Web Site: www.pnefc.net
E-Mail: enquiries@pnefc.net
League: 1st Division
Brief History: Founded 1867 as a Rugby Club, changed to soccer in 1881. Former ground: Moor Park, moved to (later named) Deepdale in 1875. Founder-members Football League (1888). Record attendance 42,684
(Total) Current Capacity: 21,363 (14,730 seated) (prior to redevelopment)
Visiting Supporters' Allocation: 5,942 maximum
Club Colours: White shirts, blue shorts

Nearest Railway Station: Preston (2 miles)
Parking (Car): West Stand car park
Parking (Coach/Bus): West Stand car park
Police Force and Tel No: Lancashire (01772 203203)
Disabled Visitors' Facilities:
Wheelchairs: Tom Finney Stand and Bill Shankly Stand
Blind: Earphones Commentary
Anticipated Development(s): Work started on the reconstruction of the Town End towards the end of the 2000/01 season; this is scheduled for completion by the start of the new season. This will be followed by the construction of the Pavilion Stand, that will see the ground's capacity reach 30,000 all-seated.

KEY
S Club Shop

⬆ North direction (approx)

❶ A6033 Deepdale Road
❷ Lawthorpe Road
❸ Car Park
❹ A5085 Blackpool Road
❺ Preston BR Station (2 miles)
❻ Bill Shankly Stand
❼ Tom Finney Stand
❽ Town End Stand (under construction

Above: 687980; *Right:* 687984

After the promotion from the Second Division at the end of 1999/2000 most fans of North End would have settled for a year of consolidation in the First Division, given that many of the pundits expected the team to struggle. However, David Moyes and his team prospered at the higher level and guaranteed themselves a place in the Play-Offs. Victory of Birmingham — in controversial circumstances — in a penalty shoot-out at a partially rebuilt Deepdale set up a final against Bolton Wanderers. Unfortunately, the final in Cardiff was a game too far, and North End came away with a 3-0 defeat. However, the success in 2000/01 bodes well for next season's campaign, provided that Moyes sticks with the team; there are strong rumours at the time of writing that he will be moving to Old Trafford. If he does so, then any new manager will have a hard act to follow.

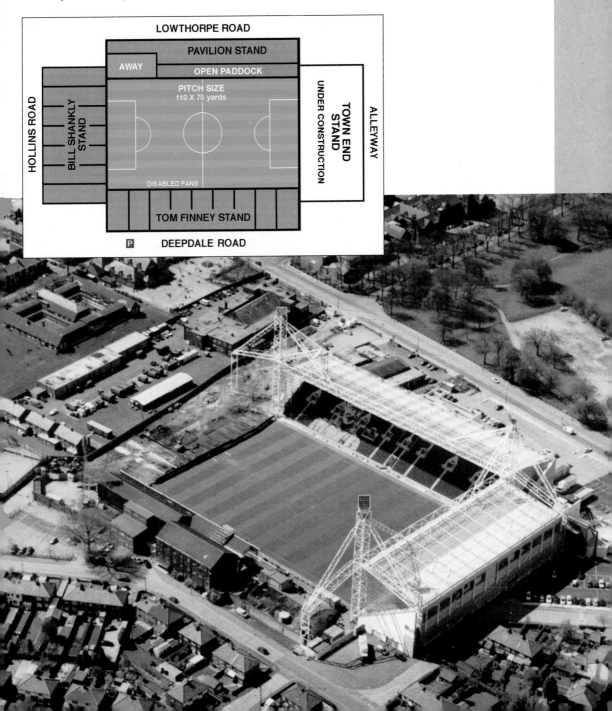

LOWTHORPE ROAD

PAVILION STAND

AWAY   OPEN PADDOCK

PITCH SIZE
110 X 75 yards

HOLLINS ROAD

BILL SHANKLY STAND

DISABLED FANS

TOWN END STAND
UNDER CONSTRUCTION

ALLEYWAY

TOM FINNEY STAND

P   DEEPDALE ROAD

QUEENS PARK RANGERS

Loftus Road Stadium, South Africa Road, London, W12 7PA

Tel No: 020 8743 0262
Advance Tickets Tel No: 020 8740 2575
Fax: 020 8740 2525
Web Site: www.qpr.co.uk
League: 2nd Division
Brief History: Founded 1885 as 'St. Jude's Institute', amalgamated with Christchurch Rangers to become Queens Park Rangers in 1886. Football League record number of former Grounds and Ground moves (13 different venues, 17 changes), including White City Stadium (twice) final move to Loftus Road in 1963. Founder-members Third Division (1920). Record attendance (at Loftus Road) 35,353

(Total) Current Capacity: 19,148 (all seated)
Visiting Supporters' Allocation: 3,100

Club Colours: Blue and white hooped shirts, white shorts
Nearest Railway Station: Shepherds Bush and White City (both tube)
Parking (Car): White City NCP and street parking
Parking (Coach/Bus): White City NCP
Police Force and Tel No: Metropolitan (020 8246 7255)
Disabled Visitors' Facilities:
  Wheelchairs: Ellerslie Road Stand and West Paddock
  Blind: Ellerslie Road Stand
Anticipated Development(s): There is vague talk of possible relocation, but nothing has been confirmed. Given the constrained site occupied by Loftus Road, it will be difficult to increase the existing ground's capacity.

KEY

C Club Offices
S Club Shop
E Entrance(s) for visiting supporters

↑ North direction (approx)

❶ South Africa Road
❷ To White City Tube Station, A219 Wood Lane and A40 Western Avenue
❸ A420 Uxbridge Road
❹ To Shepherds Bush Tube Station
❺ Ellerslie Road
❻ BBC Television Centre
❼ Loftus Road
❽ Bloemfontein Road

Deep in debt, relegation to the Second Division, financial administration and the possibility that the club may merge with Wimbledon; there is not much for the average QPR fan to look back on in the 2000/01 with pleasure. The season was always going to be a struggle for Gerry Francis and his team; the Premiership 'parachute' had come to an end and the club was not in a position to strengthen its squad significantly. The problem was then compounded by the decision of chairman Chris Wright to stand down and by Francis's departure, to be replaced by Ian Holloway. Unfortunately, the change at the top failed to reverse the club's fortunes on the field and the club was relegated to the Second Division well before the end of the season. QPR entered the close season in administration and with confirmation that there were ongoing discussions with Wimbledon about a possible merger. Whilst fans from both teams have made their opposition to such a deal evident — and the track record from other proposed mergers (remember Robert Maxwell and his scheme for Oxford United and Reading?) is not inspiring — QPR's plight is certainly a serious one. Assuming that the club survives, then it ought to threaten to achieve promotion in 2001/02, but don't hold your breath. It's all a far cry from the period in the 1990s when QPR prospered at the highest level.

SOUTH AFRICA ROAD

SOUTH AFRICA ROAD STAND

SEATED/COVERED PADDOCK

DISABLED FANS

PITCH SIZE
112 X 72 yards

BLOEMFONTEIN ROAD

SCHOOL END

AWAY

DISABLED FANS

ELLERSLIE ROAD STAND

ELLERSLIE ROAD

LOFTUS ROAD STAND

LOFTUS ROAD

LOWER

UPPER

READING

Madejski Stadium, Bennet Road, Reading, RG2 0FL

Tel No: 0118 968 1100
Advance Tickets Tel No: 0118 968 1000
Fax: 0118 968 1101
Web Site: www.readingfc.co.uk
E-Mail: comments@readingfc.co.uk
League: 2nd Division
Brief History: Founded 1871. Amalgamated with Reading Hornets in 1877 and with Earley in 1889. Former Grounds: Reading Recreation Ground, Reading Cricket Ground, Coley Park, Caversham Cricket Cround and Elm Park (1895-1998); moved to the Madejski Stadium at the start of the 1998/99 season. Founder-members of the Third Division in 1920. Record attendance (at Elm Park) 33,042; (at Madejski Stadium) 20,055
(Total) Current Capacity: 24,200 (all seated)
Visiting Supporters' Allocation: 4,300

(maximum in the South Stand)
Club Colours: White with blue hoops shirts, white shorts
Nearest Railway Station: Reading (2.5 miles)
Parking (Car): 1,800-space car park at the ground, 700 of these spaces are reserved
Parking (Coach/Bus): As directed
Police Force and Tel No: Thames Valley (0118 953 6000)
Disabled Visitors' Facilities:
  Wheelchairs: 128 designated spaces on all four sides of the ground
  Blind: 12 places for match day commentaries
Anticipated Development(s): The club has plans, if the need arises, to add an addition 5,000-seat section to the East Stand.

KEY

C Club Offices
S Club Shop

↑ North direction (approx)

❶ North Stand
❷ East Stand
❸ South Stand (away)
❹ West Stand
❺ Reading Stadium
❻ A33 Basingstoke Road
❼ To Reading town centre and station (two miles)
❽ M4 Junction (J11)
❾ Link Road to A33
❿ A33 southbound
⓫ M4 westbound (towards Swindon)
⓬ M4 eastbound (towards London)

Above: 688634; *Right:* 688627

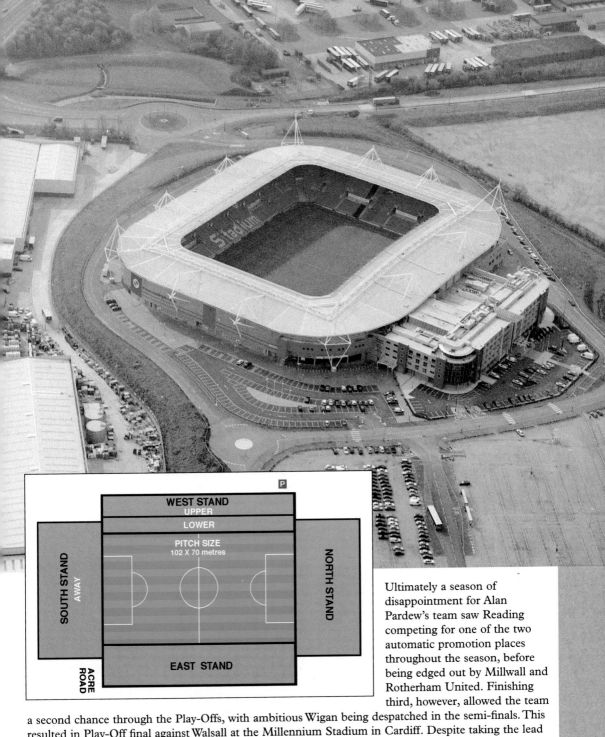

WEST STAND
UPPER

LOWER

PITCH SIZE
102 X 70 metres

SOUTH STAND
AWAY

NORTH STAND

EAST STAND

ACRE ROAD

Ultimately a season of disappointment for Alan Pardew's team saw Reading competing for one of the two automatic promotion places throughout the season, before being edged out by Millwall and Rotherham United. Finishing third, however, allowed the team a second chance through the Play-Offs, with ambitious Wigan being despatched in the semi-finals. This resulted in Play-Off final against Walsall at the Millennium Stadium in Cardiff. Despite taking the lead twice, once in normal time and once in extra time, Reading were eventually defeated 3-2, as the Saddlers scored two late goals (including an unfortunate own-goal). Thus Reading and the impressive Majedski Stadium face another year of Second Division football. The team will, no doubt, be seen as one of the pre-season favourites and fans will certainly expect the team to make another strong push towards promotion.

ROCHDALE

Willbutts Lane, Spotland, Rochdale, OL11 5DS

Tel No: 01706 644648
Advance Tickets Tel No: 01706 644648
Fax: 01706 648466
Web-site: www.rochdale-football-club.co.uk
E-Mail: club@rochdale-football-club.co.uk
League: 3rd Division
Brief History: Founded 1907 from former Rochadale Town F.C. (founded 1900). Founder-members Third Division North (1921). Record attendance 24,231
(Total) Current Capacity: 10,262 (8,342 seated) following completion of Pearl Street Stand

Visiting Supporters' Allocation: 3,650 (seated) in Willbutts Lane Stand
Club Colours: Blue shirts, blue shorts
Nearest Railway Station: Rochdale
Parking (Car): Rear of ground
Parking (Coach/Bus): Rear of ground
Police Force and Tel No: Greater Manchester (01706 647401)
Disabled Visitors' Facilities:
  Wheelchairs: Main stand – disabled area
  Blind: Commentary available
Anticipated Development(s): None following completion of Willbutts Lane Stand.

KEY

C Club Offices
S Club Shop
E Entrance(s) for visiting supporters

⬆ North direction (approx)

❶ Willbutts Lane
❷ A627 Edenfield Road
❸ Rochdale BR Station (1/2 mile)
❹ Sandy Lane
❺ To M62
❻ To M65 and North
❼ Pearl Street Stand
❽ Willbutts Lane Stand

Above: 687996; *Right:* 687986

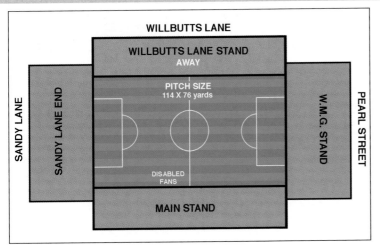

WILLBUTTS LANE

WILLBUTTS LANE STAND
AWAY

SANDY LANE

SANDY LANE END

PITCH SIZE
114 X 76 yards

DISABLED
FANS

PEARL STREET

W.M.G. STAND

MAIN STAND

Traditionally perceived as one of the Third Division's perpetual strugglers, Rochdale can count themselves unlucky in 2000/01 in that they just missed filling seventh spot by one point (and an inferior goal difference) and thus failed to get into the Play-Offs. Ironically, the beneficiaries of the last day's results — which saw Blackpool win at Darlington and Rochdale draw at Plymouth — were the Seasiders, who went on to triumph in the Play-Off final at Cardiff. With Steve Parkin still in charge, the dramatic improvements that he has wrought on the team mean that, unusually, Rochdale ought to go better in 2001/02 and achieve a Play-Off spot at worst.

ROTHERHAM UNITED

Millmoor Ground, Rotherham, S60 1HR

Tel No: 01709 512434
Advance Tickets Tel No: 01709 309440
Fax: 01709 512762
Web Site: www.themillers.co.uk
League: 1st Division
Brief History: Founded 1877 (as Thornhill later Thornhill United), changed name to Rotherham County in 1905 and to Rotherham United in 1925 (amalgamated with Rotherham Town – Football League members 1893-97 – in 1925). Former Grounds include: Red House Ground and Clifton Lane Cricket Ground, moved to Millmoor in 1907. Record attendance 25,000
(Total) Current Capacity: 11,161 (4,486 seated)
Visiting Supporters' Allocation: 2,155 (all seated) in Railway End

Club Colours: Red shirts, white shorts
Nearest Railway Station: Rotherham Central
Parking (Car): Kimberworth and Main Street car parks, plus large car park adjacent to ground
Parking (Coach/Bus): As directed by Police
Police Force and Tel No: South Yorkshire (01709 371121)
Disabled Visitors' Facilities:
  Wheelchairs: Millmoor Lane
  Blind: Commentary available
Anticipated Developments(s): The club has plans for the redevelopment of Millmoor, starting with the construction of a new Millmoor Lane Stand to be followed by a new Main Stand. There is, however, no confirmed schedule for this work.

KEY

- **C** Club Offices
- **S** Club Shop
- **E** Entrance(s) for visiting supporters
- **R** Refreshment bars for visiting supporters
- **T** Toilets for visiting supporters

↑ North direction (approx)

- ❶ Car Park
- ❷ To Rotherham Central BR Station
- ❸ A6109 Masborough Road
- ❹ Millmoor Lane
- ❺ To A6178 and M1 Junction 34

Above: 688743; *Right:* 688740

MILLMOOR LANE

OPEN TERRACE	**MILLMOOR LANE STAND**	AWAY

DISABLED FANS
PITCH SIZE
115 X 76 yards

MASBROUGH STREET

TIVOLI END COVERED TERRACE

RAILWAY END COVERED TERRACE AWAY

UNCOVERED TERRACE	**MAIN STAND** ENCLOSURE

One of the surprise packages of last season's Second Division, having been promoted from the Third at the end of the 1999/2000 season, the Millers under Ronnie Moore proved a considerable handful and, ultimately, achieved the second automatic spot to the First Division, just missing out on the Championship when results on the last day went against the club. Although the new season will bring lucrative derby matches against Sheffield Wednesday, Sheffield United and Barnsley, fans of Rotherham will be aware that, for many clubs, two promotions in two seasons is often one promotion too many. The realists will accept that anything outside the relegation zone will offer a good platform for future success, but that the club needs a season of consolidation is certain.

RUSHDEN & DIAMONDS

Nene Park, Diamond Way, Irthlingborough, NN9 5QF

Tel No: 01933 652000
Advance Tickets Tel No: 01933 652939
Fax: 01933 650418
Web Site: www.thediamondsfc.com
League: 3rd Division
Brief History: Rushden & Diamonds represents a merger between two teams — Rushden Town (founded in 1889) and Irthlingborough Diamonds (founded in 1946). The union, engineered by Max Griggs, occurred at the end of the 1991/92 season and from the start the club was based at the Nene Park ground of Irthlingborough Diamonds. Record attendance at Nene Park as a merged team 6431
(Total) Current Capacity: 6,635 (4,800 seated)
Visiting Supporters' Allocation: 1,000 seats in the north side of the East Stand

Club Colours: White with red and blue trim shirts; blue shorts
Nearest Railway Station: Wellingborough (six miles)
Parking (Car): 1,000 spaces at ground
Parking (Coach/Bus): As directed by the police
Police Force and Tel No: Northamptonshire (01604 700700)
Disabled Visitors' Facilities:
  Wheelchairs: 22 Places in the North Stand allocated to season ticket holders; 12 in the South Stand — limited number available on match by match basis
  Blind: No special facility
Anticipated Development(s): None

KEY

⬆ North direction (approx)

❶ A6 Station Road
❷ To Rushden
❸ To Kettering
❹ Station Road (old)
❺ B5348 Station Road to Irthlingborough
❻ Diamond Way
❼ River Nene

Above: 688708; *Right:* 688704

After a couple of seasons of near misses, the Brian Talbot-managed Rushden & Diamonds finally achieved Max Griggs's ambitions when they saw off the challenge of Yeovil to bring Third Division football to this corner of Northamptonshire. Widely perceived as the Man United of non-league football, the club — funded on the back of the Doc Martens' boot business — is an ambitious outfit and will almost certainly feature in the race for promotion from the Third Division. However, it may not have happened as, for much of the season, Yeovil Town were in the driving seat, with points and games in hand. Ultimately, however, Town's end of season form deteriorated markedly, with too many defeats against opposition lower in the league, and Rushden & Diamonds were to emerge as comfortable champions.

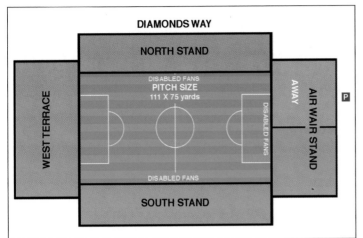

SCUNTHORPE UNITED

Glanford Park, Doncaster Road, Scunthorpe DN15 8TD

Tel No: 01724 848077
Advance Tickets Tel No: 01724 848077
Fax: 01724 857986
Web Site: www.scunthorpe-united.co.uk
E-mail: scunthorpeunited@talk21.com
League: 3rd Division
Brief History: Founded 1899 as Scunthorpe United, amalgamated with North Lindsey to become 'Scunthorpe & Lindsey United' in 1912. Changed name to Scunthorpe United in 1956. Former Grounds: Crosby (Lindsey United) and Old Showground, moved to Glanford Park in 1988. Elected to Football League in 1950. Record attendance 8,775 (23,935 at Old Showground)
(Total) Current Capacity: 9,200 (6,400 seated)
Visiting Supporters' Allocation: 1,678

Club Colours: White shirts with claret and blue trim, white shorts
Nearest Railway Station: Scunthorpe
Parking (Car): At ground
Parking (Coach/Bus): At ground
Police Force and Tel No: Humberside (01724 282888)
Disabled Visitors' Facilities:
  Wheelchairs: GMB Stand
  Blind: Commentary available
Anticipated Development(s): Although a new stadium – Glanford Park opened in 1988 – there is a possibility that, in the future, the existing Evening Telegraph Stand will be demolished and replaced by a two-tier structure.

KEY

C Club Offices
S Club Shop
E Entrance(s) for visiting supporters
R Refreshment bars for visiting supporters
T Toilets for visiting supporters

↑ North direction (approx)

❶ Car Park
❷ Evening Telegraph Stand
❸ A18 to Scunthorpe BR Station and Town Centre (1½ miles)
❹ M181 and M180 Junction 3

Above: 688732; Right: 688726

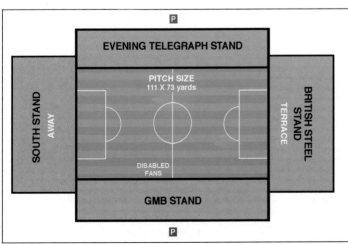

EVENING TELEGRAPH STAND

PITCH SIZE
111 X 73 yards

SOUTH STAND
AWAY

BRITISH STEEL
STAND
TERRACE

DISABLED
FANS

GMB STAND

Following relegation at the end of 1999/2000, loyal fans were expecting Brian Laws's team to make an immediate return to the Second Division in 2000/01 and many of the pundits also saw the team as being potential candidates for the Play-Offs at the very least. In the event, however, finishing in 10th place will therefore be regarded as a considerable disappointment. United is another team that should make a significant challenge in 2001/02 and will undoubtedly be amongst the pre-season favourites.

SHEFFIELD UNITED

Bramall Lane, Sheffield, S2 4SU

Tel No: 0114 221 5757
Advance Tickets Tel No: 0114 221 1889
Fax: 0114 272 3030
Web Site: http://www.sufc.co.uk
E-Mail: info@sufc.co.uk
League: 1st Division
Brief History: Founded 1889. (Sheffield Wednesday occasionally used Bramall Lane c1880.) Founder-members 2nd Division (1892). Record attendance 68,287
(Total) Current Capacity: 30,370 (all seated)
Visiting Supporters' Allocation: 2,063 (seated)
Club Colours: Red and white striped shirts, black shorts

Nearest Railway Station: Sheffield Midland
Parking (Car): Street parking
Parking (Coach/Bus): As directed by Police
Police Force and Tel No: South Yorkshire (0114 276 8522)
Disabled Visitors' Facilities:
  Wheelchairs: John Street South Stand
  Blind: Commentary available
Anticipated Development(s): None planned following the completion of the John Street Stand.

KEY

- **C** Club Offices
- **S** Club Shop
- **E** Entrance(s) for visiting supporters

⬆ North direction (approx)

- ❶ A621 Bramall Lane
- ❷ Shoreham Street
- ❸ Car Park
- ❹ Sheffield Midland BR Station (1/4 mile)
- ❺ John Street
- ❻ Spion Stand
- ❼ John Street Stand
- ❽ St Mary's Road

Above: 688043; *Right:* 688040

In the all-important local league, the Blades came out well on top, easily beating rivals Barnsley and Wednesday by finishing 10th. With Rotherham United also joining the First Division in 2001/02 the league starts to look like a South Yorkshire preserve. However, local rivalry counts for little when there is the little matter of promotion to be considered and United, whilst never in the hunt for automatic promotion, had their chances to achieve a Play-Off spot. Unfortunately these aspirations came to nothing, but the improvement over the position achieved in 1999/2000 by Neil Warnock's team bodes well for progress in 2001/02.

SHEFFIELD WEDNESDAY

Hillsborough, Sheffield, S6 1SW

Tel No: 0114 221 2121
Advance Tickets Tel No: 0114 221 2400
Fax: 0114 221 2122
Web Site: http://swfc.co.uk
E-Mail: enquiries@swfc.co.uk
League: 1st Division
Brief History: Founded 1867 as The
Wednesday F.C. (changed to Sheffield
Wednesday c1930). Former Grounds: London
Road, Wyrtle Road (Heeley), Sheaf House
Ground, Encliffe & Olive Grove (Bramall Lane
also used occasionally), moved to Hillsborough
(then named 'Owlerton' in 1899). Founder-
members Second Division (1892). Record
attendance 72,841

(Total) Current Capacity: 39,184 (all seated)
Visiting Supporters' Allocation: 3,900 (all
seated) in West Stand Upper
Club Colours: Blue and white striped shirts,
blue shorts
Nearest Railway Station: Sheffield (4 miles)
Parking (Car): Street Parking
Parking (Coach/Bus): Owlerton Stadium
Police Force and Tel No: South Yorkshire
(0114 234 3131)
Disabled Visitors' Facilities:
Wheelchairs: North and Lower West Stands
Blind: Commentary available

KEY

C Club Offices
S Club Shop
E Entrance(s) for visiting
supporters

↑ North direction (approx)

❶ Leppings Lane
❷ River Don
❸ A61 Penistone Road North
❹ Sheffield BR Station and
City Centre (4 miles)
❺ Spion Kop
❻ To M1 (North)
❼ To M1 (South)
❽ West Stand

Above: 688756; *Right:* 688754

Following the trauma of relegation at the end of the 1999/2000 season, Wednesday — a team facing huge debts and the need to reduce significantly its playing staff — poached Paul Jewell from Bradford City. Jewell, who had proved himself adept at getting considerable success with unfancied City, was, however, to prove less successful with the Owls. A series of defeats made it appear that the club was facing a second successive relegation. Desperate times need desperate measures and Jewell's departure saw the return of Peter Shreeve and an almost immediate upturn in form. Whilst fans of the Owls will regard the mid-table position that the club achieved as being a disappointment, it is a great deal better than it looked at the start of the New Year. With Shreeve now confirmed as permanent manager for the new campaign, Wednesday should be stronger candidates for a promotion push in 2001/02. However, this is the second and last season of the Premiership's 'parachute' and, given the club's financial position, 2002/03 will be a real struggle if promotion is not gained this time.

SHREWSBURY TOWN

Gay Meadow, Shrewsbury, SY2 6AB

Tel No: 01743 360111
Advance Tickets Tel No: 01743 360111
Fax: 01743 236384
Web Site: www.shrewsburytown.co.uk
E-mail: office@shrewsburytown.co.uk
League: 3rd Division
Brief History: Founded 1886. Former Gounds: Monkmoor Racecourse, Ambler's Field & The Barracks Ground (moved to Gay Meadow in 1910). Elected to Football League in 1950. Record attendance 18,917.
(Total) Current Capacity: 8,000 (4,000 seated)
Visiting Supporters' Allocation: 2,000 (500 seated)
Club Colours: Blue and amber striped shirts, blue and amber shorts
Nearest Railway Station: Shrewsbury
Parking (Car): Adjacent car park
Parking (Coach/Bus): Gay Meadow

Police Force and Tel No: West Mercia (01743 232888)
Disabled Visitors' Facilities:
  Wheelchairs: Alongside pitch (as directed)
  Blind: No special facility
Anticipated Development(s): The club is still hoping to construct a new stadium. It was hoped that work would have started on the proposed new £8.5 million ground, but problems obtaining planning permission for the new ground and for any redevelopment of the existing Gay Meadow site has yet to be forthcoming. The proposed new stadium would provide seats for about 10,000 fans. Until outstanding issues are resolved it is unlikely that the club will be able to contemplate work on the new stadium and thus the Gay Meadow is likely to be home for the Shrews for at least another season.

KEY
- **C** Club Offices
- **S** Club Shop
- **E** Entrance(s) for visiting supporters
- **R** Refreshment bars for visiting supporters
- **T** Toilets for visiting supporters

↑ North direction (approx)

❶ Entrance road to ground
❷ Abbey Foregate
❸ River Severn
❹ Car Parks
❺ Shrewsbury BR Station (1 mile – shortest route)
❻ Riverside Terrace
❼ English Bridge
❽ Wyle Cop
❾ Station End (away)
❿ Wakeman End
⓫ Wakeman/Centre/Station Stand
⓬ Old Potts Way (all routes via ring road)

Above: 679527; Right: 679522

Another nerve-wracking season for long-suffering fans of the Shrews saw Kevin Ratcliffe's team close to the Third Division drop zone. Ultimately, however, the club was to pull well away from the foot of the table, courtesy of some impressive late season form (including a 3-0 triumph at the Gay Meadow over champions Brighton) to finish in 15th position, which represented a considerable improvement over 1999/2000. The club's position was not helped during the course of the season when several home games had to be called off as a result of flooding in the River Severn. If the team can maintain the late season surge witnessed in 2000/01 then fans might have cause for optimism that 2001/02 might see the Shrews progress to the top half of the table.

SOUTHAMPTON

The Friends Provident St Mary's Stadium, Britannia Road, Southampton SO14

Tel No: 0870 22 00 000
Advance Tickets Tel No: 0870 22 00150
Fax: 02380 330360
Web Site: www.saintsfc.co.uk
E-Mail: sfc@tcp.co.uk
League: F. A. Premier
Brief History: Founded 1885 as 'Southampton St. Mary's Young Men's Association (changed name to Southampton in 1897). Former Grounds: Northlands Road, Antelope Ground, County Ground, moved to The Dell in 1898 and to St Mary's Stadium in 2001. Founder members Third Division (1920). Record attendance (at The Dell) 31,044
(Total) Current Capacity: 32,251 (all-seated)
Visiting Supporters' Allocation: c3,000 in North Stand

Club Colours: Red and white shirts, black shorts
Nearest Railway Station: Southampton
Parking (Car): Street parking or town centre car parks
Parking (Coach/Bus): As directed by the police
Police Force and Tel No: Hampshire (02380 581111)
Disabled Visitors' Facilities:
Wheelchairs: c180 places
Blind: Commentary available
Anticipated Development(s): After a number of years, planning permission was granted in 1999 for the construction of the new £32 million ground. This replaces The Dell at the start of the new season and doubles Southampton's capacity.

KEY

C Club Offices
S Club Shop
E Entrance(s) for visiting supporters
R Refreshment bars for visiting supporters
T Toilets for visiting supporters

⬆ North direction (approx)

❶ A3024 Northam Road
❷ B3028 Britannia Road
❸ River Itchen
❹ To M27 (five miles)
❺ To Southampton Central station and town centre
❻ Marine Parade
❼ To A3025 (and Itchen toll bridge)
❽ Belvedere Road

Above: 688648; *Right:* 688646

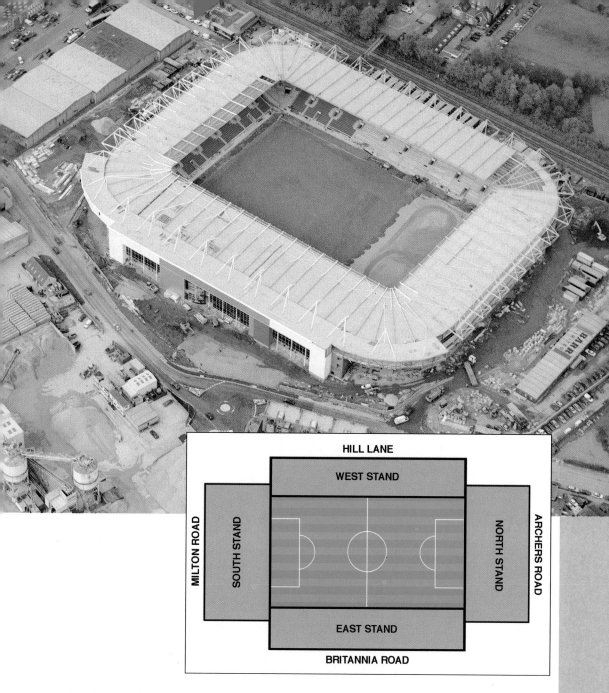

HILL LANE

WEST STAND

MILTON ROAD

SOUTH STAND

NORTH STAND

ARCHERS ROAD

EAST STAND

BRITANNIA ROAD

For their last season at The Dell, the Saints achieved the almost miraculous position of Premiership safety well before the final day's matches. Under now departed Glenn Hoddle the team looked to have an outside chance of a European place. In the event, however, a dramatic dip in form following Hoddle's move to Tottenham saw the team struggle both to score and to gain further points; in retrospect, it was probably just as well that Premiership survival was achieved before Hoddle departed. Nonetheless Southampton will launch the new ground in the Premiership; whether that status will be retained at the end of the season, however, must be a cause for doubt. High spending Fulham and ambitious Blackburn look much stronger than the teams being relegated, and this year could be the one that marks the Saints out as 'the weakest link'; much will depend on new boss Stuart Grey's ability to build upon the existing squad.

SOUTHEND UNITED

Roots Hall Ground, Victoria Avenue, Southend-on-Sea, SS2 6NQ

Tel No: 01702 304050
Advance Tickets Tel No: 01702 304090
Fax: 01702 330164
Web Site: www.southendunited.co.uk
E-mail: info@southendunited.co.uk
League: 3rd Division
Brief History: Founded 1906. Former Grounds: Roots Hall, Kursaal, the Stadium Grainger Road, moved to Roots Hall (new Ground) 1955. Founder-members Third Division (1920). Record attendance 31,033
(Total) Current Capacity: 12,306 (all seated)
Visiting Supporters' Allocation: 3,110 (all seated) in North Stand and North West Enclosure
Club Colours: Blue shirts, blue shorts

Nearest Railway Station: Prittlewell
Parking (Car): Street parking
Parking (Coach/Bus): Car park at Ground
Police Force and Tel No: Essex (01702 431212)
Disabled Visitors' Facilities:
  Wheelchairs: West Stand
  Blind: Commentary available
Anticipated Development(s): With time running out on United's occupation of the now leased Roots Hall — the club has two more years on the lease to run — the pressure is on to get progress on the proposed new stadium. Unfortunately planning permission has yet to be granted for the construction of a new ground behind the club's existing training ground at Fossetts Farm.

KEY

C Club Offices
E Entrance(s) for visiting supporters
R Refreshment bars for visiting supporters
T Toilets for visiting supporters

↑ North direction (approx)

❶ Director's Car Park
❷ Prittlewell BR Station (¼ mile)
❸ A127 Victoria Aveneue
❹ Fairfax Drive
❺ Southend centre (½ mile)
❻ North Stand

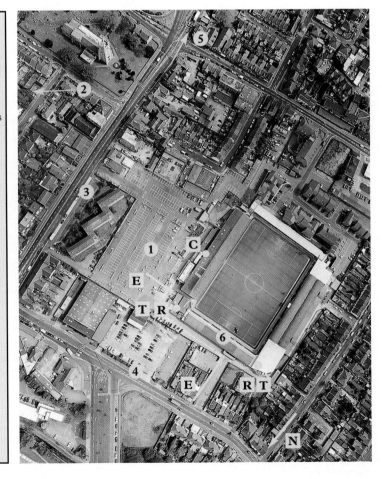

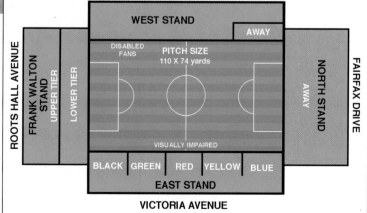

SHAKESPEARE DRIVE

WEST STAND

AWAY

DISABLED FANS

PITCH SIZE
110 X 74 yards

ROOTS HALL AVENUE

FRANK WALTON STAND

UPPER TIER

LOWER TIER

NORTH STAND

AWAY

FAIRFAX DRIVE

VISUALLY IMPAIRED

| BLACK | GREEN | RED | YELLOW | BLUE |

EAST STAND

VICTORIA AVENUE

Widely tipped for a further season of mid-table mediocrity, Alan Little's team can certainly be said to have lived up that (limited) ambition, although finishing 11th did mark a considerable advance on the 16th achieved in 1999/2000. However, with no certainty about the club's future home and with, like most lower division teams, increasing strains on financial resources, anything above 10th in 2001/02 will be seen as a considerable triumph.

STOCKPORT COUNTY

Edgeley Park, Hardcastle Road, Edgeley, Stockport, SK3 9DD

Tel No: 0161 286 8888
Advance Tickets Tel No: 0161 286 8888
Fax: 0161 286 8900
Web Site: www.stockportcounty.com
E-mail: info@iocounty.co.uk
League: 1st Division
Brief History: Founded 1883 as Heaton Norris Rovers, changed name to Stockport County in 1890. Former Grounds: Heaton Norris Recreation Ground, Heaton Norris Wanderers Cricket Ground, Chorlton's Farm, Ash Inn Ground, Wilkes Field (Belmont Street) and Nursery Inn (Green Lane), moved to Edgeley Park in 1902. Record attendance 27,833
(Total) Current Capacity: 11,761 (9,491 seated)
Visiting Supporters' Allocation: 3,615 (964 seated)
Club Colours: Blue with white stripe shirts, blue shorts
Nearest Railway Station: Stockport

Parking (Car): Street Parking
Parking (Coach/Bus): As directed by Police
Police Force and Tel No: Greater Manchester (0161 872 5050)
Disabled Visitors' Facilities:
  Wheelchairs: Main Stand
  Blind: Headsets available
Anticipated Development(s): Although the club is still planning for the reconstruction of the Railway End, with the intention of constructing a new 5,500-seat capacity stand on the site, there is no time scale for this work (which had originally been planned for 1999/2000). Theoretically, the next phase after the Railway End would be an upgrade to the Vernons BS Stand, with the intention of making the ground's capacity 20,000. The club also indicated that it might have been interested in taking over Maine Road when Manchester City move to their new stadium, but this proposal seems unlikely to proceed.

KEY

C Club Offices
E Entrance(s) for visiting supporters

↑ North direction (approx)

❶ Mercian Way
❷ Hardcastle Road
❸ Stockport BR station (1/4 mile)
❹ Railway End
❺ Main Stand
❻ Cheadle Stand

VERNON BS STAND

PITCH SIZE
111 X 71 yards

RAILWAY END
UNCOVERED TERRACE
AWAY

CHEADLE STAND

DISABLED
FANS

AWAY

MAIN STAND

P **HARDCASTLE ROAD**

Although widely considered as being likely relegation candidates and indeed being involved in the relegation battle until almost the end of the season, Andy Kilner's team managed to amass enough points to ensure that there will be a further season of First Division football at Edgeley Park in 2001/02. Unfortunately, unless there is a dramatic improvement in the team's performances during the season, fans can again look forward to a long battle to avoid the drop back to the Second Division.

STOKE CITY

Britannia Stadium, Stanley Matthews Way, Stoke-on-Trent ST4 5EG

Tel No: 01782 592222
Advance Tickets Tel No: 01782 592200
Fax: 01782 592221
Web Site: www.stokecityfc.com
League: 2nd Division
Brief History: Founded 1863 as Stoke F.C., amalgamated with Stoke Victoria in 1878, changed to Stoke City in 1925. Former Grounds: Sweetings Field, Victoria Ground (1878-1997), moved to new ground for start of 1997/98 season. Record attendance (at Victoria Ground): 51,380; at Britannia Stadium 26,664
(Total) Current Capacity: 28,083 (all-seater)
Visiting Supporters' Allocation: 4,800 (in the South Stand)
Club Colours: Red and white striped shirts, white shorts

Nearest Railway Station: Stoke-on-Trent
Parking (Car): The 650 parking spaces at the ground are for officials and guests only. The 1,600 spaces in the South car park are pre-booked only, with the majority held by season ticket holders. There is some on-street parking, but with a 10-15min walk.
Parking (Coach/Bus): As directed
Police Force and Tel No: Staffordshire (01782 744644)
Disabled Visitors' Facilities:
  Wheelchairs: 164 places for disabled spectators
  Blind: Commentaries available
Anticipated Development(s): None following the completion of the new ground.

KEY

↑ North direction (approx)

❶ Victoria Ground (site of)
❷ Stoke BR station
❸ A500 Queensway
❹ North Stand
❺ West Stand
❻ East Stand
❼ South Stand (away)
❽ A50 to Uttoxeter
❾ To M6 northbound
❿ To M6 southbound

For the second season running, Stoke City reached the Play-Offs but, as in 1999/2000, defeat over the two legs of the semi-final, this time by Walsall, ensures that the impressive Britannia Stadium will again see Second Division football during 2001/02. With the Icelander Gudjon Thordarson still in charge for the 2001/02 campaign, fans will be hoping that it is third time lucky and that one of the great clubs of English football can achieve promotion back to the First Division.

SUNDERLAND

Stadium of Light, Sunderland, SR5 1SU

Tel No: 0191 551 5000
Advance Tickets Tel No: 0191 551 5151
Fax: 0191 551 5123
Web Site: www.sunderland-afc.com
League: F.A. Premiership
Brief History: Founded 1879 as 'Sunderland & District Teachers Association', changed to 'Sunderland Association' in 1880 and shortly after to 'Sunderland'. Former Grounds: Blue House Field, Groves Field (Ashbrooke), Horatio Street, Abbs Field, Newcastle Road and Roker Park (1898-1997); moved to Stadium of Light for the start of the 1997/98 season. Record crowd (at Roker Park): 75,118; at Stadium of Light (48,285)
(Total) Current Capacity: 48,300 all-seater
Visiting Supporters' Allocation: 3,000 (South Stand)
Club Colours: Red and white striped shirts, black shorts

Nearest Railway Station: Sunderland (one mile)
Parking (Car): Car park at ground reserved for season ticket holders. Limited on-street parking (but the police may decide to introduce restrictions). Otherwise off-street parking in city centre
Parking (Coach/Bus): As directed
Police Force and Tel No: Tyne & Wear (0191 567 6155)
Disabled Visitors' Facilities:
Wheelchairs: 180 spots
Blind: Commentary available
Anticipated Development(s): Work on the £6 million expansion of the North Stand at the Stadium of Light was completed during 2000/01, taking the ground's capacity to over 48,000. This is the first phase of a three-phase scheme to increase the ground's capacity to 66,000.

KEY
C Club Offices
S Club Shop
E Entrance(s) for visiting supporters

↑ North direction (approx)

❶ River Wear
❷ North (Vaux) Stand
❸ South (Metro FM) Stand (away)
❹ To Sunderland BR station (0.5 mile)
❺ Southwick Road
❻ Stadium Way
❼ Millennium Way
❽ Hay Street
❾ To Wearmouth Bridge (via A1018 North Bridge Street) to City Centre

Above: 688659; Right: 688650

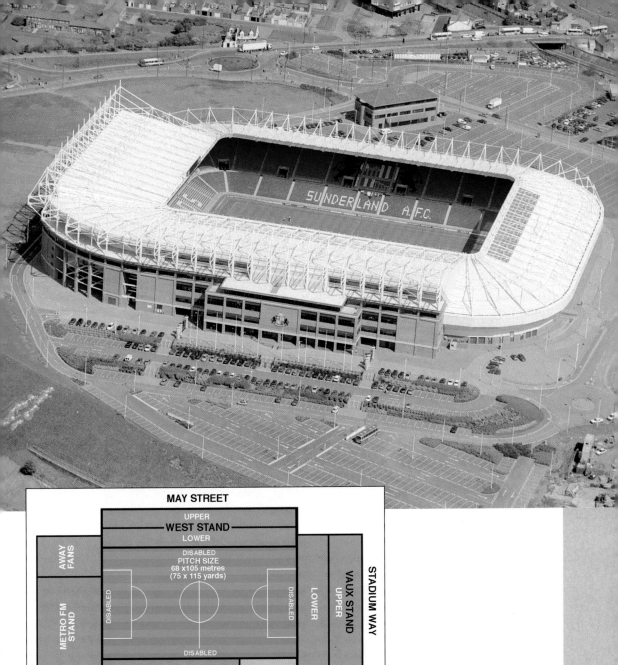

MAY STREET

UPPER
WEST STAND
LOWER

AWAY FANS

METRO FM STAND

DISABLED

DISABLED

PITCH SIZE
68 x105 metres
(75 x 115 yards)

DISABLED

DISABLED

LOWER

VAUX STAND UPPER

STADIUM WAY

McEWANS STAND

FAMILY ENCLOSURE

MILLENNIUM STAND

The second season for the Black Cats back in the Premiership again saw Peter Reid's team perform well, even if Kevin Phillips was no longer quite as productive in front of goal as he had been in 1999/2000. For much of the season it looked as though the team would finish in the UEFA Cup spots in the Premiership, thus bringing European football to the Stadium of Light for the first time, but results towards the end of the season and Chelsea's late run resulted in the London side pipping Sunderland to the all-important sixth place. However, fans can again look forward to a season of considerable promise on Wearside in 2001/02.

SWANSEA CITY

Vetch Field, Swansea SA1 3SU

Tel No: 01792 633400
Advance Tickets Tel No: 01792 633425
Fax: 01792 646120
Web Site: www.swanseacity.net
E-mail: info@swanseacity.net
League: 3rd Division
Brief History: Founded 1900 as Swansea Town, changed to Swansea City in 1970. Former Grounds: various, including Recreation Ground. Moved to Vetch Field in 1912. Founder-members Third Division (1920). Record attendance 32,796
(Total) Current Capacity: 10,420 (2,500 seated)
Visiting Supporters' Allocation: 1,541 (on the West Terrace)
Club Colours: White shirts, white shorts
Nearest Railway Station: Swansea High Street
Parking (Car): Kingsway car park and adjacent Clarence Terrace (supervised car park)
Parking (Coach/Bus): As directed by Police
Police Force and Tel No: South Wales (01792 456999)
Disabled Visitors' Facilities:
  Wheelchairs: Glamorgan Street
  Blind: No special facility
Anticipated Development(s): Plans for the construction of the new £75 million 25,000-seat stadium at Morfa were approved by Swansea Council in January 2001 with the intention that the new ground, to be used jointly by Swansea City and the city's rugby club, will available from September 2002. However, City's owners, Ninth Floor, put the club up for sale towards the end of the season and this must cause doubts as to whether the original time scale can be met. Expect the team to spend at least one further season at the Vetch Field.

KEY

C Club Offices

S Club Shop

E Entrance(s) for visiting supporters

R Refreshment bars for visiting supporters

T Toilets for visiting supporters

⬆ North direction (approx)

❶ Glamorgan Street
❷ William Street
❸ Richardson Street
❹ A4067 Oystermouth Road (8 miles to M4 Junction 42)
❺ Swansea High Street BR Station (1/2 mile)
❻ Supervised Car Park
❼ North Bank

162　　Above: 615398; Right: 615403

One of a number of clubs that no seem to lead a yo-yo existence between two divisions, this time it was relegation for the John Hollins-managed Swans as team finished a disappointing 23rd in the Second Division, with only the dire form of Oxford United keeping them off the bottom. The gall that Swans' fans will feel about this demotion will be more than compounded by the fact that arch local rivals Cardiff City will be replacing them in the Second and, in Sam Hammam, have a chairman who is clearly ambitious to take Cardiff to higher things at a time when Swansea are up for sale and have no certainly about the development of the all-important new stadium at Morfa. Undoubtedly, City be one of the pre-season favourites to make an immediate return, but much will depend on the situation off the field if these hopes are to be fulfilled.

SWINDON TOWN

County Ground, County Road, Swindon, SN1 2ED

Tel No: 01793 333700
Advance Tickets Tel No: 01793 333777
Fax: 01793 333703
Web Site: http://www.swindonfc.co.uk
League: 2nd Division
Brief History: Founded 1881. Former Grounds: Quarry Ground, Globe Road, Croft Ground, County Ground (adjacent to current Ground and now Cricket Ground), moved to current County Ground in 1896. Founder-members Third Division (1920). Record attendance 32,000.
(Total) Current Capacity: 15,165 (all seated)
Visiting Supporters' Allocation: 3,342 (all seated) in Arkell's Stand and Stratton Bank
Club Colours: Red shirts, white shorts
Nearest Railway Station: Swindon
Parking (Car): Town Centre
Parking (Coach/Bus): Adjacent car park

Police Force and Tel No: Wiltshire (01793 528111)
Disabled Visitors' Facilities:
Wheelchairs: In front of Town End and Nationwide and Arkell's stands
Blind: Commentary available
Anticipated Development(s): There remain tentative proposals for putting a roof over the Stratton End, although this is strongly opposed by local residents. The club was taken over in 2000 by millionaire Terry Brady and he had ambitious plans for the construction of a new £37 million stadium close to the M4 although there is still no definite timescale for when and if this work will take place (particularly now that Brady has relinquished the chair). Currently, only two sides of the County Ground are in use regularly, with the two ends being used for overflow capacity alone.

KEY

C Club Offices
S Club Shop
E Entrance(s) for visiting supporters
R Refreshment bars for visiting supporters
T Toilets for visiting supporters

↑ North direction (approx)

❶ Shrivenham Road
❷ County Ground
❸ A345 Queens Drive (M4 Junction 15 – 3½ miles)
❹ Swindon BR Station (½ mile)
❺ Town End
❻ Car Park
❼ County Cricket Ground
❽ Nationwide Stand
❾ Arkell's Stand

For much of the season it looked as though Swindon would fulfil the prophecies that suggested prior to the start of the 2000/01 season that the team would, like Oxford United, face an ultimately forlorn battle against relegation. However, enough points were in the bag by the final Saturday to ensure that, despite a thumping 4-1 defeat at Stoke City and a 4-0 home win for Bristol Rovers over Wrexham, Second Division football would again be on the menu at the County Ground in 2001/02. However, it is hard to escape the conclusion that a further season of struggle beckons in the new campaign and that inevitable relegation will be the view of most of the pundits.

TORQUAY UNITED

Plainmoor Ground, Torquay, TQ1 3PS

Tel No: 01803 328666
Advance Tickets Tel No: 01803 328666
Fax: 01803 323976
E-Mail: gullsfc@freeuk.com
League: 3rd Division
Brief History: Founded 1898, as Torquay
United, amalgamated with Ellacombe in 1910,
changed name to Torquay Town. Amalgamated
with Babbacombe in 1921, changed name to
Torquay United. Former Grounds:
Teignmouth Road, Torquay Recreation
Ground, Cricketfield Road & Torquay Cricket
Ground, moved to Plainmoor (Ellacombe
Ground) in 1910. Record attendance 21,908
(Total) Current Capacity: 6,003 (2,446 seated)
Visiting Supporters' Allocation: 1,004 (196
seated)
Club Colours: Yellow with white stripe shirts,
navy shorts
Nearest Railway Station: Torquay (2 miles)
Parking (Car): Street parking
Parking (Coach/Bus): Lymington Road coach
station
Police Force and Tel No: Devon & Cornwall
(01803 214491)
Disabled Visitors' Facilities:
   Wheelchairs: Ellacombe End
   Blind: Commentary available
Anticipated Development(s): There are
proposals for a joint project with a local school
for the rebuilding of the Main Stand. This
would give United a 2,500-seat stand. There
are also still plans for the redevelopment of the
Warbro End. In neither case, however, is there
a definite timescale.

KEY

C Club Offices
S Club Shop
E Entrance(s) for visiting supporters
R Refreshment bars for visiting supporters
T Toilets for visiting supporters

⬆ North direction (approx)

❶ Warbro Road
❷ B3202 Marychurch Road
❸ Marnham Road
❹ Torquay BR Station (2 miles)
❺ To A38
❻ Babbacombe End

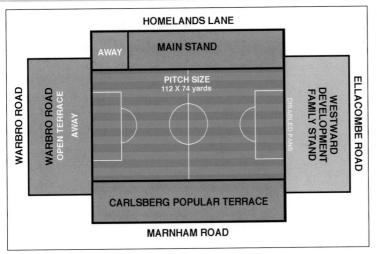

HOMELANDS LANE

AWAY | MAIN STAND

WARBRO ROAD

WARBRO ROAD OPEN TERRACE AWAY

PITCH SIZE
112 X 74 yards

DISABLED FANS

ELLACOMBE ROAD

WESTWARD DEVELOPMENT FAMILY STAND

CARLSBERG POPULAR TERRACE

MARNHAM ROAD

Last day drama does not come in a more heart-wrenching way than knowing that your final game of the season will determine whether you retain your League status or not. But that was exactly the case for Torquay and the drama was compounded by the fact that the game was away at fellow strugglers Barnet. Whoever lost was doomed to the Nationwide Conference and it all looked promising for Torquay when they swept to a 3-0 half-time lead. But Barnet came back strongly in the second half, but didn't achieve enough and were ultimately defeated 3-2. After 10 years, Barnet's Football League adventure had come to an end. Temporarily managed by ex-Wolves boss (and ex-Torquay player) Colin Lee – now departed – following the sacking of previous boss Wes Saunders in March 2001, Torquay lived to fight another year. However, the team's regular flirtation with the Conference doesn't look like ending with the victory at Barnet. Expect another season of struggle at Plainmoor.

TOTTENHAM HOTSPUR

Bill Nicholson Way, 748 High Street, Tottenham, London N17 0AP

Tel No: 0208 365 5000
Ticket Line: 08700 112222
Fax: 020 8365 5005
Web Site: www.spurs.co.uk
League: F.A. Premier
Brief History: Founded 1882 as 'Hotspur', changed name to Tottenham Hotspur in 1885. Former Grounds: Tottenham Marshes and Northumberland Park, moved to White Hart Lane in 1899. F.A. Cup winner 1901 (as a non-League club). Record attendance 75,038
(Total) Current Capacity: 36,257 (all seated)
Visiting Supporters' Allocation: 3,000 (in South Stands)
Club Colours: White shirts, navy blue shorts
Nearest Railway Station: White Hart Lane plus Seven Sisters and Manor House (tube)

Parking (Car): Street parking (min 1/4 mile from ground)
Parking (Coach/Bus): Northumberland Park coach park
Police Force and Tel No: Metropolitan (0181 801 3443)
Disabled Visitors' Facilities:
  Wheelchairs: North and South Stands (by prior arrangement)
  Blind: Commentary available
Anticipated Development(s): Following the sale of the club by Alan Sugar to ENIC, the new owners announced in early March that they were considering relocation. There is, however, no confirmed schedule for if and when this will be undertaken.

KEY

C Club Offices
S Club Shop
E Entrance(s) for visiting supporters
R Refreshment bars for visiting supporters
T Toilets for visiting supporters

⬆ North direction (approx)

❶ Park Lane
❷ A1010 High Road
❸ White Hart Lane BR station
❹ Paxton Road
❺ Worcester Avenue
❻ West Stand
❼ South Stand

The footballing equivalent of 'The Odd Couple' — Tottenham being managed by an ex-Arsenal boss — was destined, sooner or later, to end and it did during the course of the season. For fans brought up on stylish football, the transfer of David Ginola to Aston Villa was almost treasonable but, ultimately, it was not results that cost Graham his job but boardroom politics. The decision by Alan Sugar to reduce his stake in the club allowed new owners to move in and it was not long before there was a change in the managerial hot seat. The worst kept secret in football was that ex-England boss (and current Southampton manager) Glenn Hoddle would move in and so it proved. On the field, despite the fact that there was a '1' in the year, Spurs failed to reach the FA Cup final, falling at the Semi-Final stage to Arsenal whilst in the league a position of mid-table anonymity means that at least Hoddle has a reasonably secure foundation to build on for 2001/02.

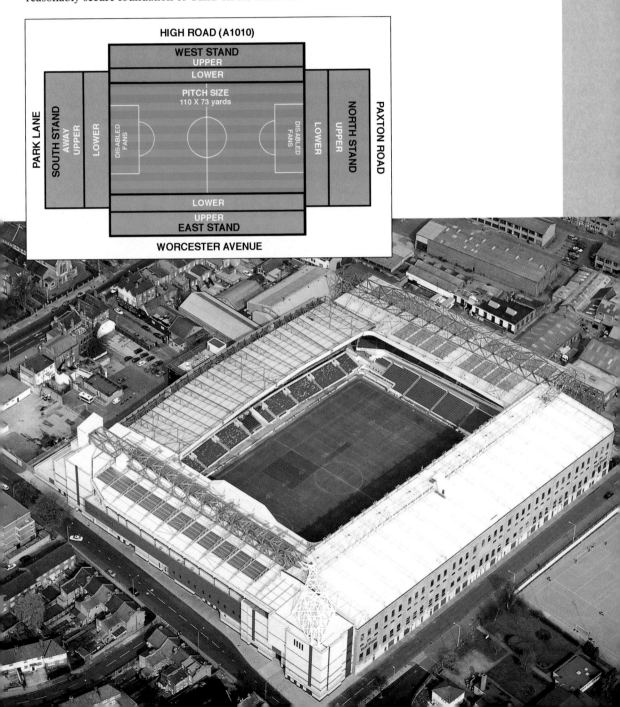

TRANMERE ROVERS

Prenton Park, Prenton Road West, Birkenhead, CH42 9PY

Tel No: 0151 609 3333
Advance Tickets Tel No: 0151 609 3322
Fax: 0151 608 4274
Web Site: http://www.tranmererovers.co.uk
League: 2nd Division
Brief History: Founded 1884 as Belmont F.C., changed name to Tranmere Rovers in 1885 (not connected to earlier 'Tranmere Rovers'). Former grounds: Steele's Field and Ravenshaw's Field (also known as Old Prenton Park, ground of Tranmere Rugby Club), moved to (new) Prenton Park in 1911. Founder-members 3rd Division North (1921). Record attendance 24,424

(Total) Current Capacity: 16,782 (all seated)
Visiting Supporters' Allocation: Between 2,000 and 5,842 (all seated)
Club Colours: White shirts, blue shorts
Nearest Railway Station: Hamilton Square or Rock Ferry
Parking (Car): Car park at Ground
Parking (Coach/Bus): Car park at Ground
Police Force and Tel No: Merseyside (0151 709 6010)
Disabled Visitors' Facilities:
　Wheelchairs: Main Stand
　Blind: Commentary available

KEY

C Club Offices

S Club Shop

E Entrance(s) for visiting supporters

R Refreshment bars for visiting supporters

T Toilets for visiting supporters

⬆ North direction (approx)

❶ Car Park
❷ Prenton Road West
❸ Borough Road
❹ M53 Junction 4 (B5151) – 3 miles
❺ Birkenhead (1 mile)

If any team during the course of the 2000/01 season can regarded as acting like Jekyll and Hyde then, without doubt, it was Tranmere Rovers. As in previous years, the team performed heroically in the cup competitions, losing only in the FA Cup to Liverpool at the Quarter-Final stage. In the league, however, it was a completely different story; dragged ultimately into the relegation mire — a series of results that cost John Aldridge the managerial hot seat — the club was never to take advantage of the games that it had in hand and was relegated to the Second Division. It seems only a couple of years ago that Tranmere were threatening to gain promotion to the Premiership; now they can look forward to local derbies against Wrexham rather than aspiring to be meeting Liverpool and Everton under new manager Dave Watson.

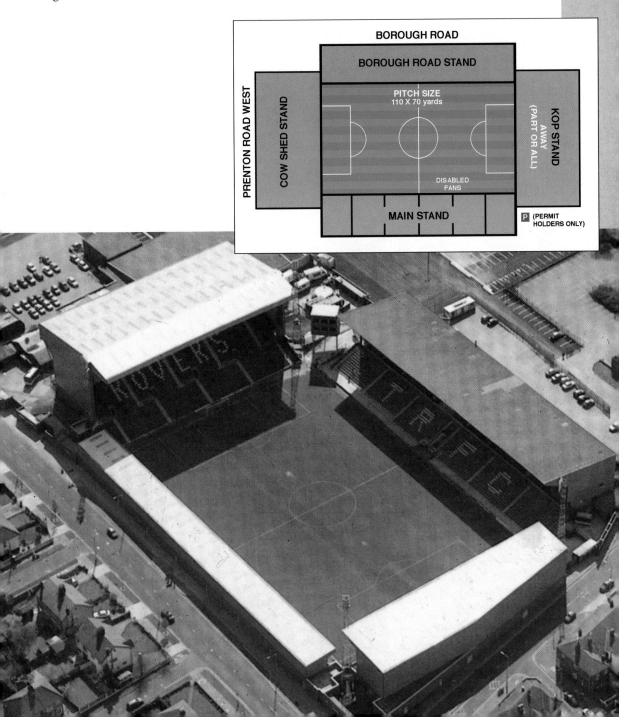

WALSALL

Bescot Stadium, Bescot Crescent, Walsall, West Midlands, WS1 4SA

Tel No: 01922 622791
Advance Tickets Tel No: 01922 651416
Fax: 01922 613202
Web Site: http://www.saddlers.co.uk/
E-Mail: wfc@saddlers.co.uk
League: 1st Division
Brief History: Founded 1888 as Walsall Town Swifts (amalgamation of Walsall Town – founded 1884 – and Walsall Swifts – founded 1885), changed name to Walsall in 1895. Former Grounds: The Chuckery, West Bromwich Road (twice), Hilary Street (later named Fellows Park, twice), moved to Bescot Stadium in 1990. Founder-members Second Division (1892). Record attendance 10,628 (25,343 at Fellows Park)
(Total) Current Capacity: 9,000 (6,700 seated)
Visiting Supporters' Allocation: 1,916 (1,916 seated)

Club Colours: Red with black shirts, black shorts
Nearest Railway Station: Bescot
Parking (Car): Car park at Ground
Parking (Coach/Bus): Car park at Ground
Police Force and Tel No: West Midlands (01922 38111)
Disabled Visitors' Facilities:
  Wheelchairs: Highgate Stand
  Blind: No special facility
Anticipated Development(s): Planning permission has been sought for the rebuilding of the Gilbert Alsop Stand, that would see the existing 2,700-capacity terrace being replaced by a two-tier 4,000-seat cantilevered stand. Works is scheduled for completion during the 2001/02 season, taking the ground's capacity to 10,500 on completion.

KEY
C Club Offices
S Club Shop
E Entrance(s) for visiting supporters
R Refreshment bars for visiting supporters
T Toilets for visiting supporters

⬆ North direction (approx)

❶ Motorway M6
❷ M6 Junction 9
❸ Bescot BR Station
❹ Car Parks
❺ Bescot Crescent

Above: 685057; *Right:* 685047

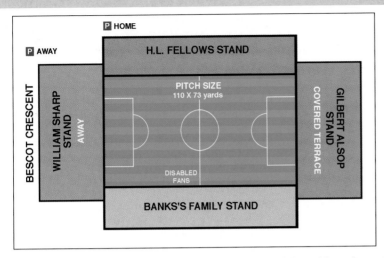

P HOME

P AWAY

H.L. FELLOWS STAND

BESCOT CRESCENT

WILLIAM SHARP STAND
AWAY

PITCH SIZE
110 X 73 yards

DISABLED
FANS

GILBERT ALSOP STAND
COVERED TERRACE

BANKS'S FAMILY STAND

Following the disappointment of the last day demotion to the Second Division at the end of the 1999/2000 season, many expected the Saddlers to make a reasonable stab at trying to regain their First Division status at the first attempt. And, under the astute management of Ray Graydon, the 2000/01 season proved to be successful. Finishing in fourth position guaranteed the team a Play-Off semi-final against Stoke City — one of the pre-season favourites for automatic promotion — which the Saddlers duly won. This was followed by a dramatic final against Reading at the Millennium Stadium. With the game tied one-all at 90min, extra time resulted with Reading again taking the lead. Two late Walsall goals, however, one of which was a freak own-goal, resulted in First Division football returning to the Bescot Stadium in 2001/02. Remembering that their team's previous sojourn at this level lasted but one year, fans will be hoping for any place higher than 19th.

WATFORD

Vicarage Road Stadium, Watford, WD1 8ER

Tel No: 01923 496000
Advance Tickets Tel No: 01923 496010
Fax: 01923 496001
Web Site: www.watfordfc.com
League: 1st Division
Brief History: Founded 1898 as an amalgamation of West Herts (founded 1891) and Watford St. Mary's (founded early 1890s). Former Grounds: Wiggenhall Road (Watford St. Mary's) and West Herts Sports Ground, moved to Vicarage Road in 1922. Founder-members Third Division (1920). Record attendance 34,009
(Total) Current Capacity: 22,763 (all seated)
Visiting Supporters' Allocation: 4,500 in Vicarage Road Stand

Club Colours: Yellow shirts, red shorts
Nearest Railway Station: Watford High Street or Watford Junction
Parking (Car): Nearby multi-storey car park in town centre (10 mins walk)
Parking (Coach/Bus): Cardiff Road car park
Police Force and Tel No: Hertfordshire (01923 244444)
Disabled Visitors' Facilities:
  Wheelchairs: Corner East Stand and South Stand (special enclosure for approx. 24 wheelchairs), plus enclosure in North East Corner
  Blind: Commentary available in the East Stand (20 seats, free of charge)

KEY

C Club Offices
S Club Shop

↑ North direction (approx)

❶ Vicarage Road
❷ Occupation Road
❸ Rous Stand
❹ Town Centre (¹/₂ mile) – Car Parks, High Street BR Station
❺ Vicarage Road Stand

Above: 688768; *Right:* 688757

Despite finishing 1999/2000 with the lowest points total ever in the Premiership, confidence was high at the start of the new season at Vicarage Road and early results seemed to justify that faith as the Hornets led the table briefly and maintained a reasonable challenge to Fulham for a period. However, in what transpired to be Graham Taylor's Swansong, the team's form deteriorated markedly and the club failed even to make the Play-Offs at the end of the season. With former Chelsea boss Gianluca Vialli appointed at the end of the season, bringing with him Ray Wilkins and Ray Lewington, it is all change at Vicarage Road at the start of 2001/02. Clearly Vialli believes the team has potential but the Hornets will probably struggle to regain Premiership status during the season.

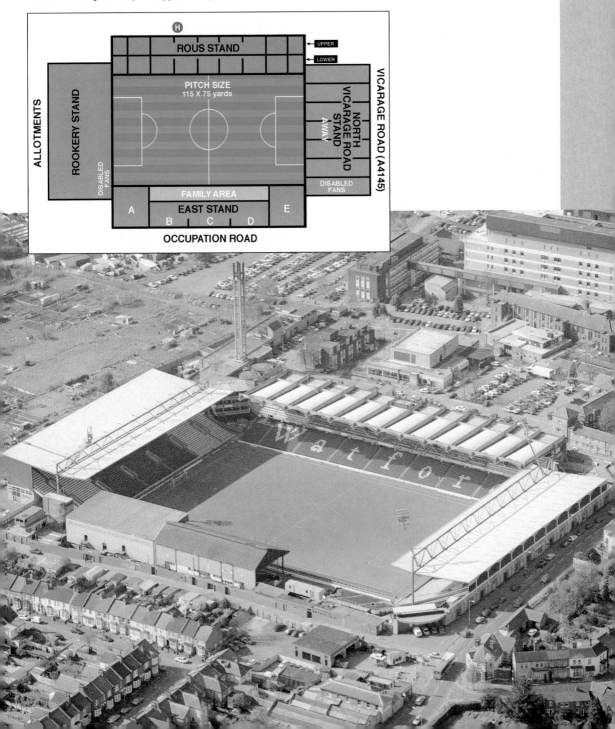

WEST BROMWICH ALBION

The Hawthorns, Halfords Lane, West Bromwich, West Midlands, B71 4LF

Tel No: 0121 525 8888
Advance Tickets Tel No: 0121 553 5472
Fax: 0121 553 6634
Web Site: www.wba.co.uk
E-Mail: enquiries@wbafc.co.uk
League: 1st Division
Brief History: Founded 1879. Former Grounds: Coopers Hill, Dartmouth Park, Four Acres, Stoney Lane, moved to the Hawthorns in 1900. Founder-members of Football League (1888). Record attendance 64,815
(Total) Current Capacity: 25,100 (all seated) (prior to redevelopment)
Visiting Supporters' Allocation: 2,100
Club Colours: Navy blue and white striped shirts, white shorts
Nearest Railway Station: Hawthorns

Parking (Car): Halfords Lane and Rainbow Stand car parks
Parking (Coach/Bus): Rainbow Stand car park
Police Force and Tel No: West Midlands (0121 554 3414
Disabled Visitors' Facilities:
  Wheelchairs: Apollo 2000 and Smethwick Road End
  Blind: Facility available
Anticipated Development(s): Planning permission was granted to allow the demolition of the 1964-built Rainbow (East) Stand in mid-January 2001. This resulted in the temporary reduction in capacity at The Hawthorns to less than 20,000. A new, 8,000-seat, stand costing £5 million, is due for completion by the start of the 2001/02 season. This will complete the planned reconstruction of the ground.

KEY

C Club Offices
S Club Shop
E Entrance(s) for visiting supporters
T Toilets for visiting supporters

North direction (approx)

❶ A41 Birmingham Road
❷ To M5 Junction 1
❸ Birmingham Centre (4 miles)
❹ Halfords Lane
❺ Main Stand
❻ Smethwick End
❼ Rolfe Street, Smethwick BR Station (1½ miles)
❽ The Hawthorns BR Station
❾ East (Rainbow) Stand (under construction)

Above: 688672; *Right:* 688662

Having survived in the First Division courtesy of results on the last day in 1999/2000, many saw the Baggies as prime candidates for relegation in 2000/01. In the event, the Gary Megson-managed team exceeded all expectations and, whilst never being in the frame for one of the two automatic promotion spots, finished in sixth place and thus entered the Play-Offs. Defeat, unfortunately, over the two legs again means that West Brom will feature in the First Division next season, but fans will be much more optimistic this year about the team's potential.

WEST HAM UNITED

Boleyn Ground, Green Street, Upton Park, London, E13 9AZ

Tel No: 020 8548 2748
Advance Tickets Tel No: 020 8548 2700
Fax: 020 8548 2758
Web Site: http://www.whufc.co.uk
League: F.A. Premiership
Brief History: Founded 1895 as Thames Ironworks, changed name to West Ham United in 1900. Former Grounds: Hermit Road, Browning Road, The Memorial Ground, moved to Boleyn Ground in 1904. Record attendance 42,322
(Total) Current Capacity: 26,052 (all seated) (prior to redevelopment)
Visiting Supporters' Allocation: 3,700
Club Colours: Claret and blue shirts, white shorts
Nearest Railway Station: Barking BR, Upton Park (tube)

Parking (Car): Street parking
Parking (Coach/Bus): As directed by Police
Police Force and Tel No: Metropolitan (020 8593 8232)
Disabled Visitors' Facilities:
  Wheelchairs: West Lower, Bobby Moore and Centenary Stands
  Blind: Commentaries available
Anticipated Development(s): Work started on the new West Stand in January 2001. It is intended that this new stand — to be called the Dr Martens Stand — will be completed by the start of the new season and see the ground's capacity increased from 26,100 to 35,000. Following this work, the club plans to rebuild the East Stand, raising the capacity to 40,000. The total cost of these new stands is £35 million.

KEY

E Entrance(s) for visiting supporters

↑ North direction (approx)

❶ A124 Barking Road
❷ Green Stree
❸ North Stand
❹ Upton Park Tube Station (1/4 mile)
❺ Barking BR Station (1 mile)
❻ Bobby Moore Stand
❼ East Stand
❽ West Stand (under construction)

Above: 688682; *Right:* 688675

A disappointing season for the Hammers in which the undoubtedly talented squad failed to live up to expectations. Widely anticipated to be amongst those chasing a European place in 2001/02, in reality, the team's initial games resulted in the side being rooted towards the bottom of the table. A mid-season revival followed when, again, a European spot seemed possible, but a late season reversal of form saw the team drift down the table again, finishing just above the relegation zone. Come the season's end, long-serving manager Harry Redknapp departed, along with Frank Lampard Snr, to be replaced by Glenn Roeder in the managerial hot-seat. These departures will probably lead to the break up of the squad, with several players, including Frank Lampard Jnr, making clear their unhappiness at the way affairs have been handled. Such is the state at West Ham, it is tempting to see the team as being one of the pre-season favourites for the drop.

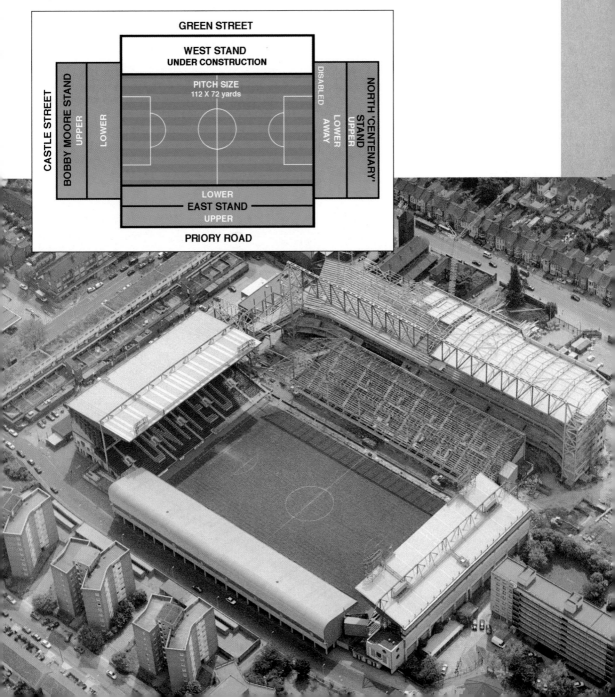

WIGAN ATHLETIC

JJB Stadium, Loire Drive, Robin Park, Wigan, Lancashire WN5 0UZ

Tel No: 01942 774000
Advance Tickets Tel No: 01942 774000
Fax: 01942 770477
Web Site: www.wiganlatics.co.uk
League: 2nd Division
Brief History: Founded 1932. Springfield Park used by former Wigan Borough (Football League 1921-1931) but unrelated to current club. Elected to Football League in 1978 (the last club to be elected rather than promoted). Moved to JJB Stadium for start of 1999/2000 season. Record attendance at Springfield Park 27,500
(Total) Current Capacity: 25,000 (all-seated)
Visiting Supporters' Allocation: 8,178 (maximum) in East Stand (all-seated)
Club Colours: White and green shirts, white and green shorts
Nearest Railway Stations: Wigan Wallgate/Wigan North Western (both about 1.5 miles away)
Parking (Car): 2,500 spaces at the ground
Parking (Coach/Bus): As directed
Police Force and Tel No: Greater Manchester (01942 244981)
Disabled Visitors' Facilities
  Wheelchairs: 100 spaces
  Blind: No special facility although it is hoped to have a system in place shortly
Anticipated Development(s): None following completion of the ground.

KEY

C Club Offices
E Entrance(s) for visiting supporters

↑ North direction (approx)

❶ Loire Drive
❷ Anjoy Boulevard
❸ Car Parks
❹ Robin Park Arena
❺ River Douglas
❻ Leeds-Liverpool Canal
❼ To A577/A49 and Wigan town centre plus Wigan (Wallgate) and Wigan (North Western) station
❽ East Stand
❾ South Stand
❿ North Stand
⓫ West Stand

Above: 685070; *Right:* 685060

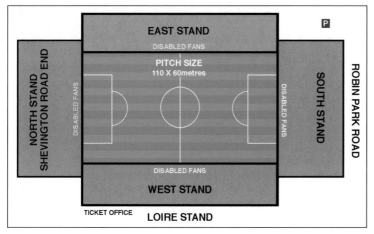

Another season, another change of manager, another near miss on the promotion stakes. Little seems to change in terms of fortune for Wigan Athletic. The season started with Bruce Rioch in charge, but he stood down in February to be replaced by the ex-Huddersfield boss Steve Bruce in early April. Under Bruce, the team again reached the Play-Offs, finishing in sixth place, but defeat over the two legs against Reading ensures that Second Division fare will again be the order of the day at the JJB Stadium in 2001/02. At the end of the season a number of familiar faces were released, including the recently signed Peter Beagrie, and the new squad for 2001/02 will again be worth regarding as good bets for the Play-Offs at the very least. Sooner or later, the pattern of the past few seasons must change surely. Bruce departed shortly after the end of the season, to be replaced by ex-Bradford City and Sheffield Wednesday boss Paul Jewell, who had some success playing for Wigan as a striker, with another ex-Bradford boss, Chris Hutchings, alongside him.

WIMBLEDON

Selhurst Park, London, SE25 6PY

Tel No: 020 8771 2233
Advance Tickets Tel No: 020 8771 8841
Fax: 020 8768 0640
Web Site: www.wimbledon-fc.co.uk
League: 1st Division
Brief History: Founded 1889 as Wimbledon Old Centrals, changed name to Wimbledon in 1905. Former Grounds: Wimbledon Common, Pepy's Road, Grand Drive, Merton Hall Road, Malden Wanderers Cricket Ground & Plough Lane. Moved to Selhurst Park (Crystal Palace F.C. Ground) in 1991. Elected to Football League in 1977. Record attendance (Plough Lane) 18,000; (Selhurst Park) 30,115
(Total) Current Capacity: 26,297 (all seated)
Visiting Supporters' Allocation: Approx 3,000
Club Colours: Blue shirts, blue shorts
Nearest Railway Station: Selhurst, Norwood Junction & Thornton Heath

Parking (Car): Street parking and Sainsbury's car park
Parking (Coach/Bus): Thornton Heath
Police Force and Tel No: Metropolitan (020 8649 1391)
Disabled Visitors' Facilities:
  Wheelchairs: Park Road
  Blind: Commentary available
Anticipated Development(s): The ongoing saga of relocation continues although, as usual, there is nothing definite to report. One possibility, opposed by the fans, is to move to a new 45,000-seat stadium being constructed at Milton Keynes. Another kite flown towards the end of the season — and soon shot down — was a merger with QPR. Expect at least another season at Selhurst Park with the rumour mill running rampant.

KEY

C Club Offices
S Club Shop
E Entrance(s) for visiting supporters
T Toilets for visiting supporters

↑ North direction (approx)

❶ Whitehorse Lane
❷ Park Road
❸ A213 Selhurst Road
❹ Selhurst BR Station (1/2 mile)
❺ Norwood Junction BR Station (1/4 mile)
❻ Thornton Heath BR Station (1/2 mile)
❼ Car Park (Sainsbury's)
❽ Holmesdale Stand

Following the despair of the last day relegation at the end of the 1999/2000 season, many expected Wimbledon to struggle in the First Division. Initially it did seem that Terry Burton's charges were going to fulfil these pre-season doubts for one very good reason — an inability to win matches at home. However, as the season progressed, so the club's position improved. Unfortunately, however, there was too much ground to be made up on either the automatic promotion places or the Play-Offs. Despite this a strong run towards the end of the season and a finishing position just outside the Play-Offs will mean that fans will view the new campaign with considerable confidence.

PARK ROAD

DISABLED

ARTHUR WAIT STAND

DISABLED FANS

WHITEHORSE LANE

WHITEHORSE LANE STAND

DISABLED FANS

PITCH SIZE
110 X 74 yards

DISABLED FANS

HOLMESDALE ROAD STAND

HOLMESDALE ROAD

MAIN STAND

WOLVERHAMPTON WANDERERS

Molineux Ground, Waterloo Road, Wolverhampton, WV1 4QR

Tel No: 01902 655000
Advance Tickets Tel No: 01902 653653
Fax: 01902 687003
Web Site: www.wolves.co.uk
E-Mail: info@wolves.co.uk
League: 1st Division
Brief History: Founded 1877 as St. Lukes, combined with Goldthorn Hill to become Wolverhampton Wanderers in 1884. Former Grounds: Old Windmill Field, John Harper's Field and Dudley Road, moved to Molineux in 1889. Founder-members Football League (1888). Record attendance 61,315
(Total) Current Capacity: 28,525 (all seated)

Visiting Supporters' Allocation: 1,500 in Jack Harris Stand or 2,971 in lower tier of John Ireland Stand
Club Colours: Gold shirts, black shorts
Nearest Railway Station: Wolverhampton
Parking (Car): West Park and adjacent North Bank
Parking (Coach/Bus): As directed by Police
Police Force and Tel No: West Midlands (01902 27851)
Disabled Visitors' Facilities:
  Wheelchairs: 164 places on two sides
  Blind: Commentary (by prior arrangement)

KEY

C Club Offices
S Club Shop
E Entrance(s) for visiting supporters
R Refreshment bars for visiting supporters
T Toilets for visiting supporters

↑ North direction (approx)

❶ Stan Cullis Stand
❷ John Ireland Stand
❸ Billy Wright Stand
❹ Ring Road – St. Peters
❺ Waterloo Road
❻ A449 Stafford Street
❼ BR Station (½ mile)
❽ Jack Harris
❾ Molineux Street
❿ Molineux Way

Another season of considerable under achievement by one of the supposed 'sleeping giants' of British football saw Wolves spend more time concerned about results in the relegation zone than battling for even a Play Off position. In the event the team's poor results cost manager Colin Lee his position. His replacement Dave Jones, the ex-Southampton and Stockport manager, knows that the scale of the job is immense and also that the expectations of the board and fans are great. With signs of dissent emerging from the dressing room from some of the high-profile players, the close season will be an opportunity for Jones to instil a sense of purpose in the squad. His successes at Stockport and at Southampton on relatively limited budgets should bode well for a club with ambition. Wolves should emerge for 2001/02 as one of the teams battling for a Play-Off place at worst; anything less will be considered a disappointment.

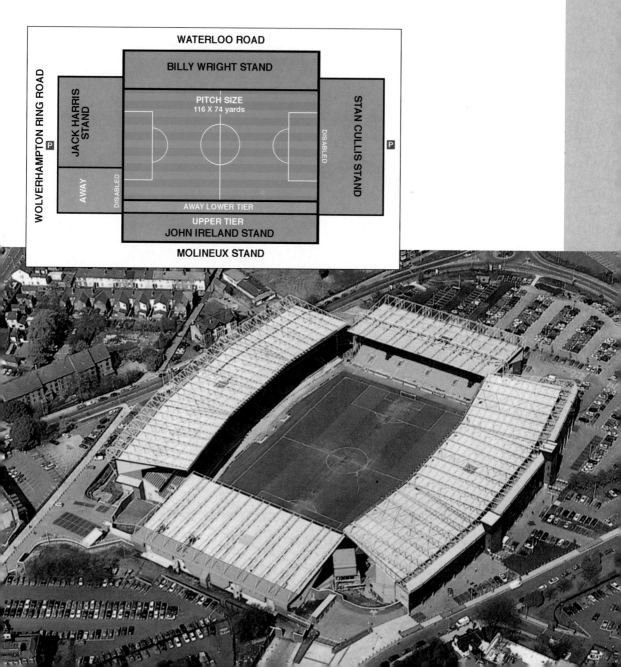

WREXHAM

Racecourse Ground, Mold Road, Wrexham, Clwyd LL11 2AN

Tel No: 01978 262129
Advance Tickets Tel No: 01978 366388
Web Site: www.wrexhamafc.co.uk
Fax: 01978 357821
League: 2nd Division
Brief History: Founded 1873 (oldest Football Club in Wales). Former Ground: Acton Park, permanent move to Racecourse Ground c.1900. Founder-members Third Division North (1921). Record attendance 34,445
(Total) Current Capacity: 15,900 (11,000 seated)
Visiting Supporters' Allocation: 3,100 (all seated)
Club Colours: Red shirts, red shorts

Nearest Railway Station: Wrexham General
Parking (Car): (Nearby) Town car parks
Parking (Coach/Bus): As directed by Police
Police Force and Tel No: Wrexham Division (01978 290222)
Disabled Visitors' Facilities:
   Wheelchairs: Mold Road Side
   Blind: No special facility
Anticipated Development(s): Following completion of the Pryce Griffiths Stand, attention will next turn to the Kop End Terrace. However, this will be retained as terracing for as long as possible and there will be no change before 2002/03 at the earliest.

KEY

C Club Offices
S Club Shop
E Entrance(s) for visiting supporters
R Refreshment bars for visiting supporters
T Toilets for visiting supporters

↑ North direction (approx)

❶ Wrexham General Station
❷ A541 – Mold Road
❸ Wrexham Town Centre
❹ Pryce Griffiths Stand
❺ Kop Town End
❻ To Wrexham Central Station

Above: 685071; *Right:* 685072

Not one of the classic seasons at the Racecourse Ground but one of consolidation for Brian Flynn's team. Variously tipped to be amongst the pack chasing a Play-Off spot or one of the also rans, Wrexham tended towards the latter, finishing in 10th place (one place better than in 1999/2000), some 12 points off the Play-Offs. The new season will see a fresh challenge for the position of being top Welsh team with Cardiff replacing Swansea in the Second Division, but fans will be expecting Wrexham to be more concerned with promotion than more parochial matters.

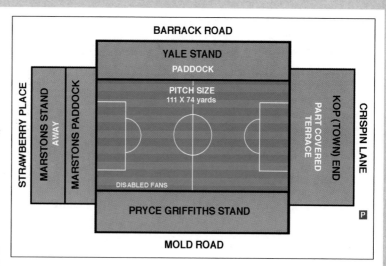

BARRACK ROAD

YALE STAND

PADDOCK

PITCH SIZE
111 X 74 yards

STRAWBERRY PLACE

MARSTONS STAND

AWAY

MARSTONS PADDOCK

DISABLED FANS

KOP (TOWN) END

PART COVERED TERRACE

CRISPIN LANE

PRYCE GRIFFITHS STAND

MOLD ROAD

P

WYCOMBE WANDERERS

Adams Park, Hillbottom Road, Sands, High Wycombe, Bucks HP12 4HJ

Tel No: 01494 472100
Advance Tickets Tel No: 01494 441118
Fax: 01494 527633
Web Site: http://wycombewanderers.co.uk
E-Mail: wwfc@wycombewanderers.co.uk
League: 2nd Division
Brief History: Founded 1884. Former Grounds:
The Rye, Spring Meadows, Loakes Park,
moved to Adams Park 1990. Promoted to
Football League 1993. Record attendance
15,678 (Loakes Park); 9,650 (Adams Park)
(Total) Current Capacity: 9,997 (7,306
seated)
Visiting Supporters' Allocation: 1,372
Club Colours: Sky blue with navy blue quartered
shirts, blue shorts
Nearest Railway Station: High Wycombe
(2½ miles)

Parking (Car): At Ground and Street parking
Parking (Coach/Bus): At Ground
Police Force and Tel No: Thames Valley
(01296 396534)
Disabled Visitors' Facilities:
Wheelchairs: Special shelter – Main Stand,
Hillbottom Road end
Blind: Commentary available
Anticipated Development(s): Although
planning permission for the expansion of the
Roger Vere Stand had been granted for some
time, work did not commence on the
reconstruction of the stand until 1 June 2001
— after the date for aerial photography for this
book was possible. It is intended that the new
stand, which will have a capacity of 2,000 when
completed, will be open early in the new season
and take Adams Park's capacity to c10,500.

KEY

C Club Offices
S Club Shop
E Entrance(s) for visiting
supporters
R Refreshment bars for visiting
supporters
T Toilets for visiting supporters

↑ North direction (approx)

❶ Car Park
❷ Hillbottom Road (Industrial
Estate)
❸ M40 Junction 4 (approx 2
miles)
❹ Wycombe Town Centre
(approx 2½ miles)
❺ Servispak Stand
❻ Roger Vere Stand (away)

Above: 688696; Right: 688685

A season of contrasts for Lawrie Sanchez and his Wycombe team: considerable success in the FA Cup but the threat, not lifted until the last few games, of relegation from the Second Division. Wycombe's successes in the FA Cup — with a home win over Wolves and an away triumph at Premiership Leicester City — brought the club a new home record crowd and, ultimately, a semi-final place against Liverpool at the newly enlarged Villa Park. Unfortunately, the team's good fortune ran out, Liverpool winning 2-1, but if the spirit that the team showed during the course of 2000/01 is reflected in the new campaign, then fans can be optimistic that the team will make better progress up the Second Division than last year.

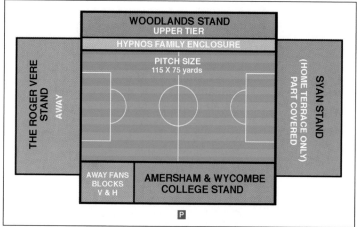

WOODLANDS STAND
UPPER TIER
HYPNOS FAMILY ENCLOSURE

THE ROGER VERE STAND
AWAY

PITCH SIZE
115 X 75 yards

SYAN STAND
(HOME TERRACE ONLY)
PART COVERED

AWAY FANS BLOCKS V & H

AMERSHAM & WYCOMBE COLLEGE STAND

P

YORK CITY

Bootham Crescent, York, YO30 7AQ

Tel No: 01904 624447
Advance Tickets Tel No: 01904 624447
Fax: 01904 631457
Web Site: www.ycfc.net
E-mail: info@ycfc.net
League: 3rd Division
Brief History: Founded 1922. Former ground: Fulfordgate Ground, moved to Bootham Crescent in 1932. Record attendance 28,123
(Total) Current Capacity: 9,606 (3,509 seated)
Visiting Supporters' Allocation: 2,380 (336 seated)

Club Colours: Red shirts, blue shorts
Nearest Railway Station: York
Parking (Car): Street parking
Parking (Coach/Bus): As directed by Police
Police Force and Tel No: North Yorkshire (01904 631321)
Disabled Visitors' Facilities:
  Wheelchairs: In front of Family Stand
  Blind: Commentary available

KEY
C Club Offices
S Club Shop
E Entrance(s) for visiting supporters
R Refreshment bars for visiting supporters
T Toilets for visiting supporters

⬆ North direction (approx)

❶ Bootham Crescent
❷ Grosvenor Road
❸ Burton Stone Lane
❹ York BR Station (1 mile)

Above: 688771; *Right:* 688770

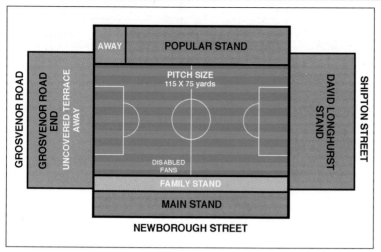

GROSVENOR ROAD

GROSVENOR ROAD END

UNCOVERED TERRACE AWAY

AWAY

POPULAR STAND

PITCH SIZE
115 X 75 yards

DISABLED FANS

FAMILY STAND

MAIN STAND

DAVID LONGHURST STAND

SHIPTON STREET

NEWBOROUGH STREET

Now managed by ex-Bradford City and Hull boss, Terry Dolan, York City never really got going in the Third Division in 2000/01 and a low mid-table position will not have satisfied the fans. Hovering just above the drop zone, but never being sucked into the last day drama, City will hope for better things come the new season.

AEROFILMS

Aerofilms was founded in 1919 and has specialised in the acquisition of aerial photography within the United Kingdom throughout its history. The company has a record of being innovative in the uses and applications of aerial photography.

Photographs looking at the environment in perspective are called oblique aerial photographs. These are taken with Hasselblad cameras by professional photographers experienced in the difficult conditions encountered in aerial work.

Photographs looking straight down are termed vertical aerial photographs. These photographs are obtained using Leica survey cameras, the products from which are normally used in the making of maps.

Aerofilms has a unique library of oblique and vertical photographs in excess of one and a half million in number covering the United Kingdom. This library of photographs dates from 1919 and is being continually updated.

Oblique and vertical photography can be taken to customers' specification by Aerofilms' professional photographers.

To discover more of the wealth of past or present photographs held in the library at Aerofilms or to commission new aerial photographs, please contact:

Aerofilms Ltd
Gate Studios
Station Road
Borehamwood
Herts WD6 1EJ

Telephone: 0208 207 0666
Fax: 0208 207 5433